GARTH BROOKS

PLATINUM COWBOY

BY EDWARD MORRIS

ST. MARTIN'S PRESS NEW YORK

Design by Judith A. Stagnitto

ISBN 0-312-08788-8

First Edition: January 1993

10 9 8 7 6 5 4 3 2 1

This book is dedicated to my precious grandchildren, Gregorio Edward Serrato and Sean Marie Della Croce, and to Garth Brooks for being a kind and generous man when those virtues were out of fashion.

ACKNOWLEDGMENTS

Of the many people who shared their notes, memories, and assessments of "what it all means" with me, I am especially indebted to Alanna Nash, Lynn Shults, Stephanie Brown, Erin Morris, Tony Byworth, Norma Morris, Debbie Holley, Dottie Witter, Jim and Trisha Harris, Susanne Woolley, Jim Della Croce, Reese Wilson, Craig Fuqua, Jim Foglesong, Bonnie Taggert, Austin Gardner, Kent Blazy, Alice Randall, Mark Renz, Sherry Bond, Don Cusic, Gerry Wood, Jason Morris, Rachel Morris, and Jody Serrato.

I also appreciate the vision and labors of my agent—how I love the sound of that phrase—Madeleine Morel (whose voice enchants even as it scolds), and my editor, the reasonably patient Jim Fitzgerald. Thanks, too, to Alex Kuczynski for keeping tabs on the project. She has been a beacon.

CONTENTS

1. Dream Chaser   1

2. Big Dreams in a Small Town   19

3. The Campus Troubadour   31

4. In Nashville to Stay   45

5. From the Deal to the Road   57

6. A New Team and a New Superstar   81

7. Garth Rules   97

8. "America's Hottest Pop Star"   121

9. What Is Brooks Singing About?   153

   Epilogue: The Hamlet of the Plains   173

   Discography   180

   Chronology   185

DREAM CHASER

It's really quite simple. All Garth Brooks wants to do is save the world and provide his friends and family with good jobs in the process. And if it's not asking too much, he would like to do this in a modest and low-key manner that befits his plain-folks image. Sure, it sounds like an impossible dream—but Brooks has proven to be an uncannily effective dreamer. Through his music, videos, and personal appearances, he has transcended mere popularity to emerge as the archetypal tough-but-tender hero America loves. Like John Denver, who vaulted across musical fences in the early 1970s, Brooks is more than a singer. In his fans' minds, he also represents visions and moral values that tower above his music. Certainly, he has the essential heroic attributes: humble beginnings, iron principles, a willingness to work hard and take risks, an abiding concern for the welfare of others, larger-than-life achievements, and a broad and endearing streak of humility. In other words, he is a very nice man flexing very large muscles.

Heroes, alas, have a habit of riding away, and Brooks may, too, when he thinks his job is done. Lately, he has talked a lot about retiring from performing and becoming a "full-time father" to his infant daughter. As extreme as such a move would be, it is entirely in character for a man whose guiding lights are neither greed nor conspicuous celebrity.

By every measure, Garth Brooks is a world-beater. Since 1989, when he released his first record, he has sold at least twenty million albums—far more than any other American act (regardless of format) during that period. He sells out every concert hall and grandstand he plays—often within a half-hour. His 1992 NBC-TV special, "This Is Garth Brooks," drew critical raves, pulled down record ratings, and, judging from the spurt in record sales immediately following the broadcast, earned him tens of thousands of new fans. He has won virtually every major award for which he has been eligible from the Academy of Country Music and the Country Music Association. His face has beamed out from the covers of *Time, Forbes, Life, USA Weekend,* and *The Saturday Evening Post;* and the tabloids regularly chronicle his marital woes and parental joys.

By conservative estimate, Brooks has generated at least half a *billion* dollars for the entertainment industry during his brief career through the sale of albums, concert tickets, home videos, and merchandise, and from music-publishing and product-licensing royalties. *Forbes* listed him as the thirteenth highest-paid entertainer in America for 1991–92, with an estimated income of forty-four millon dollars. The only country music personality in the ranking, he outpaces such other megastars as Arnold Schwarzenegger, Eddie Murphy, Tom Cruise, and Mel Gibson.

Because his influence has been so profound, Brooks can take most of the credit for liberating country music from the second-class citizenship under which it has forever been burdened. Eddie Arnold, Dolly Parton, Johnny Cash, Kenny Rogers, Glen Campbell, Anne Murray, Jimmy Dean, Roy Clark, Willie Nelson, Alabama, Randy Travis, and a few others made substantial inroads into the mass audience during their heydays; but none did it as quickly and overwhelmingly as Brooks. Their successes tended to be judged against those of other country acts. Brooks, however, has found himself pitted against the likes of Michael Jackson, Bruce

Springsteen, Hammer, Metallica, U-2, and Guns N' Roses. And he has left them all in the dust.

There will always be people who won't like country music, but from now on it will be difficult for anyone to dismiss the music as the illiterate yammerings of poor hillbillies. Because of the respect—and money—it has earned, country music now boasts some of the most skilled and perceptive music makers in existence. Under the Brooks banner, country music has become fashionable. And it has found audiences it used to concede to other musical formats—teenagers and young adults who are affluent and relatively well educated. Best of all, from Brooks's and Nashville's point of view, it has achieved that wide acceptance without forsaking the elements that make country music distinct from other kinds: an emphasis on lyrics and melody and a focus on rural and small-town life and people who live in a state of comparative innocence.

To work his cross-cultural wonders, Brooks has had to run counter to some of the more rigid conventions of country music. Although he can hoot and honky-tonk with the best of country's traditional performers—as he does, for example, in "Friends in Low Places"—he has a passion for addressing larger and more philosophical issues with his music. And his stage shows have the flash, energy, and abandon more common to rock than country. Politically, country music tends to be conservative and intolerant. Yet Brooks's "We Shall Be Free" is the boldest and broadest state-

ment on behalf of the world's despised and downtrod-
den since Bob Dylan's "Blowin' in the Wind." The song
advocates not only giving to the poor and protecting
the earth, it also lobbies for the acceptance of interracial and homosexual relationships. This degree of
openness is hard to find in any contemporary music
and unheard of in country.

So who is Garth Brooks? And what has enabled
him to take country music to a higher level of appreci-
ation than it has ever had before?

Well, we can begin with the observation that he
was born in 1962. That date implies a couple of important things. To begin with, it means that he grew up
when the first great waves of rock 'n' roll were receding, both in artistic vitality and in social impact.
Because the rock of the 1950s and 1960s was so closely identified with the growing pains of youth, it is
tempting for those who came of age in that period to
believe that rock inevitably equates with youth. Not so.
By the time young Garth Brooks was buying his first
albums and going to his first concerts, the rock of Elvis
Presley and the Beatles must have seemed closer to his
parents' generation than his own. He had no chrono-
logically vested interest in rock music. He was free to
take it or leave it, in whole or in part. Like the children
of the 1950s who turned away from the treacly pop
music of the time, Brooks in the 1970s had the same
freedom to reject the noxious and self-
indulgent elements of rock.

Furthermore, when Brooks was in
junior high and high school, American

GARTH BROOKS radio was a veritable cafeteria of sounds to savor: from the earnest and introspective ballads of James Taylor, Cat Stevens, and Dan Fogelberg to the buoyant and socially aware lyrics of John Denver, from the mindless discomania of the Bee Gees to the country/pop warblings of Crystal Gayle and Kenny Rogers. Besides these day-in, day-out musical influences, Brooks had five siblings and a mother and father at home, all of whom played their own generationally distinctive records for him to overhear. Brooks thus grew up surrounded by musical variety, but arbitrarily tied to no one style.

He did little more than dabble in music while he was in high school, but it was evident fairly early that he was developing a marvelously mobile voice—one that was bell-clear, relatively uncluttered by affectations and capable of soaring to emotionally compelling high notes. It was, as well, a voice ideally suited to conveying the one-to-one intimacy he found so alluring in Taylor's and Fogelberg's songs.

By the time he reached college, Brooks was already consumed by his love of music. He became skilled on the acoustic guitar and constantly added to his already extensive repertoire. While still an undergraduate at Oklahoma State University, he earned a campus-wide reputation as both a singer and songwriter. Those who performed or buddied with him confirm that he was an intense and magnetic presence even then. Brooks says he converted to country music in 1981 when he heard George Strait's first single,

"Unwound." He did not restrict himself to the country format, though, until he settled in Nashville in 1987.

It is no accident that the two biggest country acts of the past decade—Garth Brooks and Alabama—got their basic training singing in clubs where the patrons demanded to hear all kinds of music. These unforgiving training grounds taught performers that if they wanted to make money from the crowd, they first had to capture its attention with their stage presence and then hold it with their versatility. Brooks is fond of saying that he never had to "pay dues" to get where he is today. But the truth is that by the time he got his record deal, he could look back on seven tough years of apprenticeship.

Brooks projects such a humble and self-effacing image that it is easy to forget that he is both intelligent and well educated. And he brings all his considerable skills to bear in reaching out to people. The dramatic pitch of his speaking voice, the radiant intensity of his stare, and the effortless precision of his hand gestures all convey a sense of intimacy that transforms strangers into confidants. Whether he guides himself according to the principles he learned in his marketing and advertising classes at OSU or whether it is something etched into his instincts by years of audience feedback, Brooks has developed an extraordinary sensitivity to what the moment and the crowd require.

At the core of Brooks's appeal is the astounding sense of self he projects. He seems comfortable with his outlook on life, the values he expresses, and the way he looks. He doesn't surround himself with sycophants and toadies to demonstrate to the world that he is a big deal. In Nashville he often goes to restaurants and industry gatherings by himself or with just his wife and close friends. He is utterly free of the self-protective, self-aggrandizing pretense that is the stock-in-trade of other celebrities. People feel in him a person who won't bully or be bullied.

Says his producer, Allen Reynolds, "I've never worked with anyone who was this fully formed when I met them, in terms of their artistic maturity and their sense of self and their talent."

No doubt a great deal of Brooks's self-assurance comes from the people around him. He is doggedly loyal to those who liked him and supported him when he was a nobody, commercially speaking. And he has rewarded them well.

His older sister, Betsy Smittle, plays bass in his band. Although she had performed with the country singer Gus Hardin before Brooks got into the music business, she was not a stellar instrumentalist. Primarily, she was a vocalist and guitarist and admits that she didn't even know how to play bass when her kid brother hired her. Similarly, Kelly Brooks, Garth's older brother, knew little of the music industry at the time Garth appointed him tour manager. Before that, he had been a bank auditor. Brooks made his boyhood friend Mick Weber his road manager and gave his college roommate Ty England a slot in his band as guitarist.

Bob Doyle, Brooks's co-manager and publisher, dates back to the singer's first few weeks in Nashville. Brooks continues to write songs with people he met when he was new to the business, even though all the older established writers in Nashville would happily write with him now. Brooks is so loyal to his friends that he even butted heads with Jimmy Bowen, the powerful president of his own record company. Bowen, who runs Liberty Records (formerly Capitol/Nashville), clearly helped Brooks become the star he is today. Early on, he strongly suggested that Brooks drop Bob Doyle and Pam Lewis as his managers, arguing that they were too new to management to give him the guidance he deserved. Brooks refused. And at a memorable photo session during one of his many No. 1 parties, Brooks quietly insisted that Lynn Shults, the man who signed him to Capitol Records, pose in a group shot along with Bowen, even though Bowen had fired Shults when he took over the record label.

Joe Harris, Brooks's booking agent, signed the young singer even before he had a record contract. It is now common practice for performers to take over their own booking when they become superstars to save the percentages they would otherwise pay an agency. Randy Travis, Reba McEntire, and George Strait are all booked by their own companies. But Brooks— who these days is so wildly popular he could book himself with an answering machine— shows no signs of turning his back on Joe Harris, or on any of the other people who took a chance on him when he was starting out.

Bobby Wood and Mark Casstevens are studio musicians who have played on all of Brooks's albums. In many of his interviews, Brooks has credited his musicians for turning ordinary songs into something magical. It is Wood's distinctive piano stylings, for instance, that gives "The Dance" its classical elegance. On Brooks's Christmas album, *Beyond the Season,* he includes a Wood/Casstevens instrumental composition, "Mary's Dream." If the album sells just three million copies—and odds are it will sell many more—that one song will earn Wood and Casstevens and their publishing companies $187,500.

Brooks never undervalues the importance of individuals. Almost everyone who meets him seems to sense that. He routinely dazzles entertainment journalists, a group that prides itself on cynicism. "I've seen very few [performers] who could bond like that," says a writer who's covered the music industry for thirty years. "His eyes lock right on you, and he has you within thirty to forty-five seconds." The writer guesses that Brooks reads and listens widely in his spare time and is thus able to find common grounds for "intimate" conversation with anyone he meets.

Another key to Brooks's popularity is his love of women. That love goes well beyond the sexual attraction and fascination most men feel. Brooks adores women for what they are—not as the stylized earth mothers/sex machines they're so often reduced to. He likes to know what women are thinking and why, and he respects what he hears. It is understandable, then, why so many women are drawn to him and are wholly undeterred by the receding hairline or expanding waistline to which Brooks, himself, draws attention.

"Women are so cool," Brooks proclaimed to *USA Weekend,* "and as different as snowflakes. You can be with seven or eight women and get seven or eight sides of what a woman is. Women are neat. They're enticing." While this rapturous outburst hardly captures Brooks's understanding of women, it does show something about his level of enthusiasm for them.

"He's wholesome, he's polite, and he loves women," says Colleen Brooks, the singer's mother. "He puts women on a pedestal, and the only way they get off is to knock themselves off. He idolizes women. He wrote a song that I hope I'll talk him into recording. [It goes], 'Next to Jesus Christ, himself, a woman's the best thing that's walked on this earth.'" Susanne Woolley, a college friend, recalls that Brooks used to talk to her about how he wanted to have daughters if he ever married.

"I was always a mama's boy," Brooks says, "and still am. I just liked hanging around girls." He adds that he was in college before he really understood "how to react around guys—to *be* one of the guys."

One of Brooks's first co-writers in Nashville was a woman, Stephanie Brown. And he has since written with several other women, including his wife. Brooks had women co-writers on such popular (and lucrative) singles as

12 "The River" (Victoria Shaw) and "We Shall Be Free" (Stephanie Davis). Women are generally treated respectfully in country songs, but Brooks seems especially at ease with them in his music, neither being intimidated by them nor taking them for granted as fixtures in a male world.

Since Brooks became a big enough name to headline concerts, he has chosen women to be his opening acts: his old friend Trisha Yearwood in 1991, and his production manager's wife, Martina McBride, in 1992. Of course, both women are superb singers and quite capable of carrying the responsibilities Brooks gave them.

In a way, Brooks has developed into the country Alan Alda, a sensitive, attentive man who enjoys women at every stage from the conversational to the sexual.

In an interview with the writer Alanna Nash, Brooks tried to put into words why he found lovemaking and music making equally glorious and intense experiences:

> I just think that when you see a beautiful woman—and she doesn't have to be beautiful [in the usual sense]—just talking with her and falling in love with her, there's this drive. You can't explain this drive. You don't know. It's the same thing with music. It's that drive to make love with music—so wild, and like any good sex, the wilder and frenzier it gets,

and the quicker you can turn that around to just gentle, tender, slow and keep your partner off balance, and then smack it with something just wild and crazy again, and just keep doing that over and over until one of you drops dead, that's great physical sex. That's also great, physically feeling with music each night.

As many close to him have pointed out—and as evident in his music, videos, and album notes—Brooks has a dark, brooding side, one that dwells on loss and death. That is not surprising, given his impressionable nature. He seems to see the deaths of others as symbolic rather than statistical. He was almost killed himself in a car wreck during his senior year in college, along with Mickey Weber and another friend. But the events that put him on what seems to be a perpetual death watch were the separate accidents that killed Jim Kelley and Heidi Miller.

"Jim was a guitar player and hurdler," Brooks told *The Gavin Report*. "He was my brother Kelly's coach.... Jim was like a best friend to both of us. He was a real family man, loved his folks, and he was a pilot. He and his brother would fly home to see their mom and dad all the time. They got killed flying home to see their parents. All of a sudden, I realized what I had and how quickly I could lose it."

Heidi Miller was a fellow student and one of Brooks's first and most ardent fans: "She was probably one of my greatest

14

friends. We actually roomed together one summer. I needed a place to live, and she and another lady needed another roommate to make rent. Sandy loved them both, too. Heidi would come to every place I played, no matter how far away, no matter what.... Well, Heidi met this wonderful man and fell in love with him. [She] was ten days from graduating when a drunk driver hit them head on. She was killed instantly."

Brooks dedicated his first album "to the loving memories" of these two friends.

"If Tomorrow Never Comes," Brooks's second single and first video, implicitly took up the death theme—not as a tragedy to dwell on but as a reality by which to judge one's current conduct toward loved ones.

It was his video for "The Dance," however, that focused on the untimely deaths of heroic figures to preach the message of nothing ventured, nothing gained: "I could have missed the pain," says the chorus, "but I'd have had to miss the dance." At the most superficial level, the song is about taking a chance on love. To Brooks, though, it was about taking a chance on life. And to make this point vividly, he used footage of people who had died in the process of risking great things: Martin Luther King, Jr., John F. Kennedy, John Wayne, the crew of the ill-fated Challenger space craft, rodeo champion Lane Frost, and country singer Keith Whitley. Brooks intensified the already emotionally taut video by adding a spoken introduction and conclusion.

To teenagers, whose half-child/half-adult lives are intrinsically melodramatic, "The Dance" was a weighty message, indeed. It told them exactly what they needed to hear: seize the day. And it also resonated profoundly to traditional country music listeners, who are used to drama and sentimentality in their songs. If there was a single crucial element in Brooks's rise to superstardom, it was surely this video. It showed a somber, caring, thoughtful, all-embracing male toward whom only positives applied.

"The Dance" video was later compiled into a package with Brooks's other two videos, "If Tomorrow Never Comes" and "The Thunder Rolls." In his commentary on "The Dance" for this project, Brooks explained his fascination with the song by noting, "If I had to trade one yesterday so I could have one tomorrow, I don't think I could."

In another reference to dying young, Brooks recalled the first time he heard his first single, "Much Too Young (to Feel This Damn Old)," on the radio. He said he was in Nashville, driving home from a writing appointment, when the song came on. He was so excited, he continued, that he turned up the sound and started driving as fast as his truck would go. When the song was over, he punched in another country station—and it was also playing his song. At this point, he said that he thought it would be all right if he wrecked, because he was "at the top."

When eight members of Reba McEntire's entourage died in a charter airplane crash in March of 1991, Brooks and his band wore black armbands during their concerts for the rest of the year. *Ropin' the Wind* is dedicated to "Reba's 'Crazy Eight.'"

Brooks dedicated *The Chase* to a rancher friend, the late Dale Wehr: "I will always remember what you taught me about building barns, hauling hay, and horses. What I remember most, however, I'm not sure you intended to teach me. Those who fear death are the same ones who have not lived their lives to the fullest; when you laughed in death's face, you were not being courageous, you were just being honest."

Remarkably, Brooks seems not to link death with his Christianity. There is none of the dying-as-a-transition-to-a-better-life theme that afflicts so much of country music. That may be because Brooks can't imagine a better life than he's living now; or it may suggest that his frequent references to "God" and "Jesus" are as much a way of keeping himself in scale as it is to celebrate a clearly perceived divinity. When he thanked God for doing "a hell of a lot for me" at the Country Music Association's award show, it was as if he were recognizing a particularly gifted co-writer.

How can the sincerely modest Brooks acknowledge his unparalleled achievements and impact without seeming egotistical? He has to confront such praise and fawning every day that if he were to let the sheer volume of it go to his head, he might try waltzing on water. It is a problem that could derail a less balanced artist, but Brooks has turned it into an image-making bonus.

Why is he rich and famous? Well, he explains, God has been good to him. Why is his music so popular? Well, it's not really his doing, you see, it's country music generally that's hot. How does it feel to have all those young lovelies leering up at him onstage? Well, they're really getting off on the lead guitarist. He has elevated self-effacement to an art form. Before he melts under the praise, he deflects it to those around him.

If Brooks were to bow out of the business now, he would have already earned the gratitude of the whole country music industry. More significant, however, is the difference he has made in the lives of those who never get any closer to philosophical rumination than listening to "The Dance" or "The River" or who may be bored by politics but susceptible to the call for decency Brooks issues in "We Shall Be Free."

In a twinkling moment of humor-coated truth, Brooks once observed: "You can't say you can't please all the people all the time until you've tried."

How he tried and how he did it are in the accounts that follow.

BIG DREAMS IN A SMALL TOWN

Oklahoma, Garth Brooks's home state, is second only to Texas as a breeding ground for world-beating country and pop singers. Its success stories are almost as common (and frequently as rich) as its oil wells. The state's green hills and brown plains have produced—to stir only the cream—

GARTH BROOKS

Leon Russell, Patti Page, Roger Miller, Reba McEntire, Spade Cooley, Vince Gill, B. J. Thomas, Wanda Jackson, Becky Hobbs, Joe Diffie, Cal Smith, and three-fourths of Restless Heart. Thus, the prospect that an Okie from a backwater town might set the musical world on its ear is not all that far-fetched. It isn't just idle boosterism that the welcoming signs at the state's borders read "Discover the Excellence."

Garth Brooks, his four brothers, and his one sister were all born in Tulsa. When Brooks was four years old, the family moved from Tulsa to Yukon, then a town with about ten thousand residents. Although it has a modest economic life of its own, Yukon is primarily a bedroom community for people who work in Oklahoma City, fifteen miles to the southeast. From the early 1970s onward, many families moved from multiracial Oklahoma City to nearly all-white Yukon to avoid mandatory busing of their children.

Partly because there are no high hills to slow down the winds or forests to moderate the temperature, Yukon gets a steady assault of hard weather. Summer days are commonly in the sweltering nineties. The winters, viewed statistically, sound almost balmy. Temperatures average in the thirties and snowfall logs in at around nine inches a year. But the winds are so fierce that the region is often raked with blizzards. It is easy to see why storms pound incessantly through Brooks's lyrics.

Not long after Brooks joined Capitol Records in 1988, the label produced a "video bio" to introduce him to the media. In it, the singer describes "the town where I was raised" in a droll talking blues song. He sums it up by saying the town had "a church, and a mill and Chuck's Conoco" and adds that the "houses were simple, but they weren't no shacks/We lived on the south side of them railroad tracks/And that 3:05 would pull in at 4 o'clock on the nose."

The town's population has doubled since Troyal and Collen Brooks moved their family there, but it still has basically the same unhurried and self-assured character.

Officially, Yukon dates back to 1891, when Czech immigrants named and incorporated the town. Even today, the Czech influence is evident, with surnames like Yanda, Stejskal, Benda, Krshka, and Kouba dotting the phone directory. In 1966, the year the Brooks family relocated, the town sponsored its first Czech Festival, an event now held every October.

Of greater historical impact to the region, however, is the fact that the Chisholm Trail—fabled in song, story and B-movies—once snaked its way through the area that would become Yukon. Between 1867 and 1887 cowboys drove more than a million longhorn cattle up from Goliad and San Marcos, Texas, across the rolling grasslands of central Oklahoma and into the railroad loading yards at Abilene, Kansas. A segment of the trail lies less than a mile from Brooks's boyhood home.

Not surprisingly, the vivid cowboy lore the Trail generated has found its way into both Brooks's stage image and the songs he writes and records: "Cowboy Bill" and "Much Too Young (to Feel This Damn Old)" on his first album, *Wild Horses,* and

"Wolves" on *No Fences,* "Rodeo," "Against the Grain," and "In Lonesome Dove" on *Ropin' the Wind,* and "Night Rider's Lament" on *The Chase.*

Outwardly, though, little of the frontier lingers in Yukon. What with its McDonald's, Dairy Queen, Ace Hardware, State Farm, Wal-Mart, and Texaco, it looks very much like any other overgrown village in Ohio, Georgia, or New York. You can walk the length of Main Street and never see a cowboy hat. You will, however, see a sign at the city limits—where Route 270 becomes Main Street—that says, WELCOME TO YUKON HOME OF GARTH BROOKS. The same proud claim is painted on one of the town's water towers. Like most small towns, Yukon dotes on native sons and daughters who bring fame—and the tourist dollars that go with it.

Yukon's four-lane Main Street runs east and west through the business district on the town's northern edge. Most of the stores, fast-food joints, and office buildings are one- or two-story brick and cinder-block affairs. But the row of tall, bone-white cylindrical silos of the MFC Farmers Co-op give the town a skyline, as does the looming and clifflike Yukon's Best Flour mill directly across the street. Because of its wheat-processing industry, the Yukon high school teams are called the Millers.

High school sports are such a big deal in Yukon, says one longtime resident, that "you could have a big murder in town, and it probably wouldn't be as big a story as what the football score was."

The citizens are served by two local newspapers: the twice-a-week *Review* and the weekly *Sun*. Of late, Brooks's mother has been writing an occasional entertainment column for the *Sun*. It's called "By Brooks' Side" and for the most part deals, quite understandably, with the activities of her youngest son.

Brooks grew up in a split-level brick house at 408 Yukon Avenue, eight blocks south of Main Street and only a few minutes' walk from the high school. The two- and three-bedroom homes along the street have tiny, well-tended front lawns and slightly larger backyards. The short driveway at the Brooks house leads to the one-car garage where Garth used to play games, daydream, and practice his music. The windows in the rooms above the garage look onto the street through blue ornamental shutters. A low row of shrubbery coils along the front entrance, and there are a few small trees in back of the house. If a movie company wanted a pleasant suburban neighborhood setting for a film about the innocent 1950s, it could do no better than this.

In his NBC-TV special, Brooks waxed lyrical about his boyhood home. It was a house that was "just totally cool," he rhapsodized. "You could live in the house. You could try things—stretch your imagination. It was a house you could make mistakes in."

Brooks's parents had been previously married. Troyal had a son from his first marriage; Colleen had two sons and a daughter from hers. Together, the couple had Kelly, and then, eighteen months later, Garth. Troyal

PLATINUM COWBOY

23

Brooks still works as a draftsman for the Union of California (Union 76) oil company, a job he has held since before Garth was born. "We weren't a poor, poor family," Colleen Brooks says, "but we'd scrape the bottom of the barrel a lot of times." In spite of that, she points out, "five of the kids have their [college] degree." (Betsy, who now plays bass in Garth's band, went to college for one day, her mother reports, didn't like it, and quit.) Brothers Jim and Mike are teachers, Jerry is an investigator for a public defender's office, and Betsy and Kelly work for Garth.

A happy side effect of the family's limited budget was that the children spent a lot of time entertaining themselves and each other. Three nights a week, the family would have "funny nights," during which each child would sing songs, tell jokes, or do a skit. "Garth would come up with some of the darnedest stuff you ever heard in your life—from the time he was still in diapers," Colleen Brooks recalls.

According to Mrs. Brooks, her youngest son was an amusing mimic as well. She says that his first complete sentence was "I'm the boss around here," a remark he picked up from his frequently exasperated father.

Two years after moving to Yukon, young Garth Brooks enrolled at Central Elementary School on Oak Avenue and Seventh Street. It was a safe and easy six-block walk from his house. During "Garth Brooks Day," in 1991, the singer's third-grade teacher, Pearl Kinsey, recalled that the youngster loved music—and that girls loved him. "I never had any discipline problems with Garth," she told a reporter. "The only problem I had was that I couldn't keep all the little girls away from Garth."

Although religious sentiments have become a prominent part of Brooks's public image, his mother, who was raised a Catholic, says the family did not attend church. Nonetheless, she insists that her son's interest in religion is sincere and fairly longstanding: "When Kelly and Garth were at OSU, they had the whole athletic dorm returning thanks [at meals]."

Sports, particularly baseball, were a part of the Brooks family routine. All the children were athletic to one degree or another, and Troyal Brooks coached Little League teams. Garth credits his father with endowing him with his competitive instincts. His father's message was not that Garth always had to win but that he should always try his hardest to. Anything less was self-betrayal, was unworthy. As Garth summarizes it, "I've always been raised that no matter what you do, if you're not out to be the best, don't go out there and do it."

Brooks's parents were pickers and singers, and they passed on their enthusiasm for music to the rest of the family. Troyal sang and picked the guitar, strictly as a pastime. But Colleen had spent several years seriously pursuing a career in music and still showed some of the fire during Brooks's formative period.

As a young woman in the mid-1950s, she performed briefly on Red Foley's "Ozark Jubilee" television show in

Springfield, Missouri. She also recorded a few songs during that period, notably "No Tellin'," "Bluebonnet Waltz," and "Lo Ciento Mucho." Ultimately, though, she abandoned her dream of stardom in order to raise her children; but she continued to sing publicly now and then until after her youngest was in school.

As Garth explained to the British journalist Tony Byworth, his home was a melting pot of musical styles: "My oldest brother was not that far separated from my mom and dad—like fourteen or fifteen years. So there was never really any generation gap. It was like eight people's influences of music all coming down to this last child." He says his mother listened to Harry Belafonte "a lot" and to Grand Ole Opry star Jack Greene. His sister and the oldest of his brothers favored such acts as Rita Coolidge, Janis Joplin, Townes Van Zandt, Tom Rush, Three Dog Night, and Steppenwolf. And the brothers closer to him in age listened to Boston, Journey, and Kansas. Garth, in turn, was drawn to the music of ELO, Styx, and such singer/songwriters as James Taylor, Dan Fogelberg, Elton John, and Billy Joel.

For the most part, though, Brooks just listened and absorbed. He was in high school before he began making his own music. And he was in college before it occurred to him that he might actually make a living at this melodious trade.

When he was sixteen, he got a banjo as a birthday present. That gave him something to work with.

But the stimulus that really activated his dreams

was going to concerts and watching such groups as Kiss and Queen drive audiences to a frenzy with their stabbing lights, swirls of smoke, cocky posturings, and ear-shattering volume. This was more than music, he concluded; it was also the Super Bowl, a revival meeting, and great sex compressed into wild bursts of sight and sound. It demanded everything and it gave everything. It was precisely what Brooks would offer to his own audiences of true believers in the years to come. But it would take some practice.

During Brooks's middle to late teens, disco was still throbbing in the American psyche. This was the leisure-suited era of "Stayin' Alive," "Last Dance," "How Deep Is Your Love," and "Y.M.C.A." At the more melodic end of the spectrum Brooks heard such ballads and love songs as "Hotel California," "Shower the People," "Your Smiling Face," "How Much I Feel," "Just the Way You Are," and "Sometimes When We Touch."

Country and pop were being homogenized on the radio: Crystal Gayle's "Don't It Make My Brown Eyes Blue," Dolly Parton's "Here You Come Again," Glen Campbell's "Southern Nights," and Anne Murray's "You Needed Me" were all No. 1 Top 40 hits during that period. Significantly, this was also a time of heroic, against-the-odds pop songs: the themes from *Star Wars* and *Rocky*, "Fly Like an Eagle," "We Are the Champions," and "I Will Survive." Even rough country rocker Charlie Daniels scored a pop hit in 1979 by telling, in "The Devil Went Down to Georgia," how a young fiddler triumphed over Satan. It is not difficult to see how such stirring hymns to personal heroism might affect Brooks's concept of life. As his wide repertoire as a bar singer later showed, he had been taking it all in.

"If I could have picked anybody in school who would have done what Garth has," says Reese Wilson, "it wouldn't have been him." Wilson lived three blocks away from Brooks in Yukon and went to school with him at both Central Elementary and Yukon High. As a budding rock guitarist in high school, it was Wilson, not Brooks, who seemed more likely to be a star-in-embryo. Wilson says that Brooks showed relatively little interest in music during most of his high school years. "He started later than we did. We were all ready to play music, and he was just learning what was going on. Garth was kind of a jock. And when he did get into music, it was mainly rock. When I first heard Garth on the radio, I wasn't sure it was the same guy."

But Jacque Weber, who runs the beauty shop in Yukon that Collen Brooks frequents and whose son, Mickey, is now Garth's road manager, remembers it all a bit differently:

"When the kids were in the ninth grade, Garth was always trying to get little bands together. He had an electric guitar and one amp. Mickey had a guitar but no amp. And a friend of theirs had a cymbal but no drums or drumsticks. They would sit in Mickey's bedroom. Garth would play these chords and try to teach Mickey how to play his guitar. He would plug into the amp, then unplug himself and plug Mickey in. And here's their friend Mark, sitting there with his cymbal and a pencil and trying to keep time. It was too cute."

Before he finished high school, Weber says, Garth had put together a bluegrass band and had taught her son the basics of guitar and banjo.

In spite of the town's simple charms—or more likely because of them—Reese Wilson says he and his friends found Yukon boring during their high school years. "We usually would go to Oklahoma City for entertainment because there was nothing to do in Yukon. Nothing."

Ah, yes, but what a splendid place to daydream.

CHAPTER THREE

THE CAMPUS TROUBADOUR

Garth Brooks graduated from Yukon High School in 1980 and straightaway enrolled at Oklahoma State University in Stillwater on a track scholarship. Already, though, music had become as alluring to him as athletics. Even allowing for the inevitable pangs of homesickness that accompanied his leaving the nest, Stillwater was still a comfortable place for Brooks to be. Kelly, his older brother, was already a student there, and the town was within a couple of hours' driving time from Yukon. Yet it was far enough away from his family and friends to make Brooks begin stretching out on his own.

In a very real sense, the town would become Brooks's spiritual home. It was where he would cultivate his most enduring friendships, experiment with musical styles, develop his stage persona, learn the business elements of his trade, and meet the woman who had the strength to make him stick with his dreams. Stillwater is where he returned to lick his wounds and polish his craft after his first disheartening trip to Nashville. And it gave him a name for his band. Stillwater travels with him.

OSU is a spacious, tree-lined island of activity in the middle of a town that is, in turn, surrounded by farms and ranches. It is several miles from the nearest interstate highway. Since its founding in 1890 as Oklahoma Agriculture and Mechanical College, the school has grown to attract a student population of twenty thousand. The campus is composed chiefly of uniform rows of red brick buildings and acres of well-tended gardens and lawns.

Brooks took up residence in Iba Hall, an athletic dormitory named for Henry "Hank" Iba, OSU's legendary head basketball coach and three times coach of the U.S. Olympic basketball team.

During his first year, Brooks did most of his

singing and playing in his room, often jamming with other students. In the spring of his sophomore year, he was picked to represent Iba Hall in a campus-wide talent contest for dorm residents. The contest was held April 6 in the Student Union's Little Theatre. Craig Fuqua, now a reporter for the Stillwater *NewsPress,* promoted the event and remembers how Brooks won the fifty-dollar first prize: "He sang three Dan Fogelberg songs, and he sounded pretty much like him. I believe all the songs were from Fogelberg's *The Innocent Age* album."

Fuqua's friend Susanne Woolley helped him stage the talent show. She could already vouch for Brooks's singing talents. A violinist and fiddler, she had earlier struck up a musical acquaintance with Brooks at the urging of hometown friends who lived in Brooks's dorm. "So a couple of times," she says, "we played for brown bag lunches [on campus] and once at the courthouse. We had a lot of interesting gigs." When Brooks auditioned for the talent show, she recalls, "He came in and sat down and just knocked everybody else out. It was obvious he had one of the most beautiful voices around."

Although Woolley and Brooks never dated, she says he did reveal a sensitive side that extended well beyond the lyrics he sang. "My mom and dad had four girls. We didn't have any brothers. And Garth once told me, 'Your dad must be the luckiest person in the world. I hope when I get married I get to have four daughters, too.' I remember he was always hoping he would have girls he could sing to and take care of." Jim Harris, an OSU psych major who often jammed with Brooks, recalls that one of his more memorable original songs was about "the daughter he was going to have one day."

Woolley says that when she and Brooks went to campus parties, people would always clamor for him to sing his original songs. "He and I used to talk about songwriting. That's always an intimate thing to talk to a person about because generally they reveal themselves in their songs." (Woolley, by the way, now has another Brooks tie-in. Her violin teacher's son, Dave Gant, is Brooks's keyboardist and fiddle player.)

Jim Harris says he first met Brooks at the "Aunt Molly's Rent-Free Music Emporium," an amateur-night extravanganza staged at the massive OSU Student Union on Friday nights. After the two got to know each other, Harris would sometimes stop by Brooks's dorm room and play mandolin in the communal picking sessions. Now and then, he would also sit in with Brooks on a club date. "My background is kind of bluegrass and country," Harris says. "He was doing a little bit of country, but a lot of it was easy-listening stuff." Other stalwarts at the jam sessions, Harris says, were Ty England, Brooks's roommate and now his guitarist, and the banjo player Dale Pierce.

Harris says that Brooks's sports, studies, and music kept him "on the go constantly."

From their first meeting, Harris was impressed by Brooks's guitar playing: "He could chord around on the mandolin and banjo, but the acoustic guitar was his main thing. He knew thousands of chords. He didn't take the lead that much [in playing]. Most of what he did was rhythm. But a lot of the songs he sang back then—like those by Cat Stevens and others along that line—had some pretty difficult chord patterns. So he had to have that down."

As Trisha Harris, Jim's wife, remembers it, Brooks always had the opportunity at OSU to surround himself with adoring women. But she says he seldom did: "He would stand on his stage just with his guitar and sing songs that made every girl absolutely melt. We used to play on the Aunt Molly shows with him, and when he'd get through, about ten girls would just stand there. I would get embarrassed for them. He mesmerized people." Trisha says that Brooks never dated anyone during this period, then adds, "Well, I'm sure he did some—but he never had a girlfriend then that he was obviously dating steadily."

Memories of Brooks's athletic achievements at OSU are considerably harder to find. If you call the sports information office at the school to ask for specific Brooks data, you are likely to be met with a polite silence and the clear implication that you are barking up the wrong tree.

"He was the type of kid," says OSU's track coach Dick Weis, "who was fast—but not fast enough; and he was strong—but not strong enough." Weis, who coached Brooks during his last two years in college, reveals that the scholarship student's best javelin throws were around 215 feet—"Not bad but not great." But, Weis continues, "he was always a hard worker, and he competed very hard."

By the time Jim Harris graduated in 1983, he says Brooks was "really getting on a [musical] roll" around Stillwater—not just as a soloist but also playing with The Skinner Brothers band, a country group known for its "really upbeat tunes."

In early 1984 Brooks called Harris at his home in Bartlesville, Oklahoma, and asked him if he would play on a demo session. Brooks said he wanted to make a tape to take to Nashville. To help Harris prepare, Brooks sent him a "work tape" of the songs he wanted to record. Harris doesn't remember the name of the place where the demos were made, but he describes it as "a full-fledged recording studio in the sticks east of Stillwater." Brooks also commandeered the services of Dale Pierce, several members of a country band from Claremore, Oklahoma, and some women harmony singers.

Harris still has Brooks's work tape. The songs on it are not labeled, but he says one is "Heaven Must Have a Hell of a Band," another "Claremore, Oklahoma, USA," and the third is one "about how you have to treat ladies with respect."

During the weekend recording session, Harris and his fiancée, Trisha, stayed with Pierce in his trailer. It was here that Trisha first heard Brooks sing his song about the daughter he hoped to have. In May she and Harris were married. Brooks and Ty England drove up to Bartlesville for the wedding and stayed on to play at the reception. At Trisha's request Brooks sang the daughter song again. Accompanying Brooks to the wedding was his new girlfriend, Sandy Mahl.

To earn money for the considerable expenses his scholarship and musical gigs weren't covering, Brooks worked as a bouncer at the Tumbleweed Ballroom during his senior year. Located just outside of downtown Stillwater on Country Club Road, Tumbleweed is a giant metal building that looks like an overgrown farm equipment shed. Adding to the farm aura is the fenced-in rodeo area in back of the club. Unglamorous as it may be, however, Tumbleweed is both a performance venue for major touring acts and a popular night spot for OSU students who need to shake the civilized confines of campus and boogie like real blue-collar folks. As has been told countless times, Brooks broke up a fight Sandy seemed to be winning and eventually parlayed this chance encounter into romance, marriage, and parenthood.

Sandy Mahl came to OSU from the small town of Owasso, near Tulsa. Originally, she aimed to become a physical education teacher, but then she switched her major to sociology. Two years younger than Brooks, she came to the university when he was already well on his way to becoming a local star. During Garth's last year as an undergraduate, he and Sandy moved in together, but they would not marry until after he had made his first demoralizing trip to Nashville.

Brooks completed his credits for an advertising degree and graduated from OSU in December 1984. Now with a few years of performance under his belt, a demo tape of his original songs, and the good wishes of the dozens of friends who believed in his talents, Brooks was ready to dazzle Music City. And he was going to do it by himself. Some time in 1985—the exact date is not emblazoned in Nashville history—Brooks packed most of his possessions into a Honda Accord and set out to make history. "When I left Oklahoma, when I crossed into Arkansas," Brooks recounts dramatically, "I said, 'Good-bye, Oklahoma, I don't need you. I don't need the woman that I left behind. I don't need anybody. I'm gonna make it on my own.'" But he would soon be heading back home, almost before his personal declaration of indepedence stopped echoing.

Brooks is usually short on details when it comes to describing what he actually did during his twenty-three or twenty-four hours in Nashville. But in an interview published in *The Gavin Report,* a radio trade magazine, he spelled it all out:

> I had an appointment to see Merlin Littlefield [the associate director of ASCAP, an organization that collects royalties for its songwriter members], and he sat me down and told me that my two choices were to starve as a songwriter or go out as an artist and starve with eight other people. While I was with Merlin, there was this call that so-and-so was in the lobby. He told me, "Great, you're going to see one of the greatest writers in Nashville."

So this guy comes in and tells Merlin he's having trouble paying off a $500 loan. When he left, I said, "Merlin, that guy was kidding you, wasn't he?" He says, "No, that's really how it is." I said, "Merlin, I make that in a week back home." And he said, "Go back home." I walked away from there hating Merlin's guts, but every day I thank God that he said what he said. Nashville was not the place for me then.

Brooks's feeling of instant defeat may also have had something to do with his operating alone for the first time in his life—with no older brother or sister to run interference, no friends or girlfriend to bolster his spirits, and no one to see him as anything different from the hundred other ersatz cowboys roaming down Music Row with their guitars.

"I came to Nashville thinking that opportunity just hung on trees," Brooks told the writer Tony Byworth, "and that all I had to do was take out my guitar and strum a little bit and sing and someone would say, 'Hey, kid, let me give you a record deal and a couple million dollars, and you can go back home.' That was really naive. I don't want to call it stupid. It's just naive....It's just a dream everybody has."

With his dream thoroughly canceled, Brooks sped back to Stillwater and Sandy and enrolled in a master's degree program. He was not soured on singing and writing, but he knew he'd better have something to fall back on if the music business was as tough to crack as it seemed to be. During the next two years, Brooks organized Santa Fe, a country band that toured around the region. He also got himself a Wednesday night solo gig at Willie's on "the Strip" near campus. It was here that he hardened and polished himself for his next assault on Nashville.

On Brooks's 1992 NBC-TV special, Sandy related that Brooks was paid one hundred dollars for each of his weekly four-hour sets at Willie's. His shows, she added, were pretty basic: "He would just get up in whatever he had on—his sweats, his jeans, his T-shirt, and baseball cap. At that time, he had long hair ... and a full beard and mustache. And he would just get up, and he would play anything from Neil Young to Willie Nelson, Elton John, Billy Joel, Dan Fogelberg. It was whatever anybody could yell out."

Unlike Yukon, Stillwater has never felt the impulse to memorialize its most famous former citizen. There are no signs marking Brooks's old haunts. His likeness is not hung in the Student Union, nor has the campus bookstore become a Brookstore. The campus publicity office maintains a few clippings about his achievements, but the files are hardly bulging. Locally, the chief point of pride is Eskimo Joe's, a T-shirt store and restaurant. The Eskimo Joe T-shirts, say the locals, are second in world popularity only to those bearing the logo of the Hard Rock Cafe.

If you meander along the two-block section of Washington Street called "the Strip," however, you will find people who are still in touch with the native son.

And you will see essentially the same landscape he left five years earlier.

The Strip—with its fast-food joints, T-shirt stores, bookstalls, restaurants and bars—looks exactly like every other strip near every other campus in the known universe. Lest you forget that you are in intellectual territory, there are the requisite reminders. For instance, the servers at Antonio's restaurant wear T-shirts emblazoned with an Ayn Rand quotation: "My philosophy, in essence, is the concept of man as a heroic being, with his own happiness as the moral purpose of his life, with productive achievement as his noblest activity and reason as his only absolute." Try a topping of that on your pizza.

Directly across Washington Street from Antonio's is an establishment with mercifully fewer philosophical pretensions—a place where neither man nor woman is required (or expected) to be heroic. Willie's Saloon, according to Dollye Bloodworth, who operates the bar with her husband, Bill, was Brooks's launching pad to stardom. The Bloodworths also helped Brooks make his first Nashville trip, Dollye says, although she does not offer specifics. Bill Bloodworth says he's pretty much quit talking to reporters about Brooks: "The last time somebody came to me, they made the comment, 'Boy, I need to find some real dirt.' Shit, I don't want to be involved in that. I don't want to be misquoted. Garth's a good friend of mine."

Willie's has taken on the same mythic proportions in the Garth Brooks saga that the Bowery in Myrtle Beach did in Alabama's up-from-obscurity story. Both saloons were

GARTH
42
BROOKS

testing grounds on which an act had either to triumph or retreat. In spite of its longhorn-shaped logo and weathered wood exterior, Willie's is not a country music bar, nor was it when Brooks played there. On a recent spring evening, just as the Class of '92 was about to stumble onto a bleak job market, the bar exhibited a nice balance of musical formats, with a Nashville Network show flickering silently on the TV behind the bar and Rush and Van Morrison burbling over the sound system.

Tourists in search of Garth lore or Garth spoor need not stop at Willie's. Already, the trail has grown cold. A bartender apologizes for having no stories to tell about Brooks. She adds the gratuitously painful information that she was too young to get into the pub when he played there. Merchandise emblazoned with the Willie's logo abounds—T-shirts, sweatshirts, caps, and beer can holders. But there is no Garth memorabilia, not even a sign proclaiming that he once palpitated coed hearts on this very spot.

The stage Brooks worked from is directly across the room from the bar and at the right of the door as you enter. It is roughly the size of a parking space and about eight inches higher than the rest of the floor. Standing there, Brooks could look out into a vaguely L-shaped room, packed with a dozen or so gritty-topped dining tables, two heavily used pool tables, and an ever-changing tableaux of lust on the hoof. It is not a retreat for professors who want to quietly discuss the tormenting ambiguities of Kierkegaard. But you couldn't pick a better spot to perfect your musical crowd control.

A couple of doors down from Antonio's and diagonally across the street from Willie's is DuPree's Sports Equipment store. Brooks labored here for two years when he was an undergraduate. "He was playing at the Holiday Inn here," explains the owner, Eddie Watkins, "and one of my employees said, 'Hey, Eddie, you like country and western music. You ought to go out and listen to this guy.'" Watkins took the underling's advice and quickly became a regular at Brooks's Friday and Saturday night shows. "I got to be pretty good friends with him. He'd play just about anything you asked him to do. He was really good at sounding like other artists, like Merle Haggard or George Jones."

Watkins says that Brooks admitted that he was having trouble "making ends meet," what with the hit-and-miss nature of the gigs he was doing. "I hired him. He worked for us approximately two or two and a half years prior to when he actually went to Nashville [for the first time]." Brooks knew how to handle customers, even as a sales clerk, Watkins recalls: "It was almost comical. People would come in to return a pair of shoes or something like that, and Garth would say, 'Hey, pardner, we'll get you a new pair. No problem.' "

Brooks also had a great knack for remembering people's names and faces. "That probably has to do with all the words he remembers in his songs," Watkins speculates. "The guy can sit down and sing a hundred songs in one night and not have a piece of music in front of him."

GARTH BROOKS

Historians will also be pleased to learn that long before the world at large heard about Garth Brooks, he was already outfitted to tour it. As Watkins explains it, "He was playing at Willie's, and we did a T-shirt for fun that said 'Garth Brooks World Tour' on it. All the employees were wearing them here and when they went over to Willie's."

Watkins's support and friendship for the struggling young artist has not been forgotten. In 1991 Brooks & Company were selling around sixty to seventy thousand dollars' worth of T-shirts and related merchandise at every concert, a "substantial" portion of which was purchased from Watkins. But the payback hasn't stopped there. Brooks is likely to give DuPree's a free plug at the drop of a hat—or rather at the donning of one. "We've got a hat with our logo on it," Watkins says, "and it seems like he wears it every chance he gets." (The logo is of a duck wearing a baseball cap.) Brooks wore the hat for a full-page photo in *Entertainment Weekly.* And as if that weren't enough free advertising for his old friend, Brooks subsequently popped up with the hat on his NBC-TV special.

Like the Bloodworths, Watkins says he's been hounded by tabloid reporters in pursuit of Brooks's dark side. "They were just really almost mad when they walked out of here without picking up any dirt. We've been inundated with this kind of people. But the thing is, there's just nothing that you can say bad about him. People on TV see him and probably think it's a put-on about how much he honors his parents and Sandy. But that's the way Garth is."

CHAPTER FOUR

IN NASH-VILLE TO STAY

When Garth Brooks made his second and final pilgrimage to Nashville in 1987, he had the good fortune to encounter Stephanie Brown. As it turned out, it was a lucky day for her, too. A former English teacher, Brown was herself learning the intricate craft of country songwriting. At the same time, she was keeping a close eye on the Byzantine ways of Nashville's music business.

Brooks actually made a number of forays into Nashville in 1987, all in preparation for relocating there from Stillwater. On this particular late summer trip, he came without his wife and stayed at the home of Bob Childers, an Oklahoma transplant with whom Stephanie Brown was writing.

The night following Brooks's arrival, he, Childers, and Brown went to Windows on the Cumberland, a small listening room on Nashville's trendy Second Avenue that served as a gathering place for singers, songwriters, and poets. That evening, the house was holding a "writers night." The best-known performer on the bill was Kevin Welch, an established singer/songwriter who now records for Reprise Records. Later in the evening, at Childers's urging, Brooks performed a song for the small audience. "I heard enough to know he was really good," Brown recalls.

Childers had just written a song called "It Ain't All in the Luck of the Draw," and Brown, functioning as his critic, told him she thought the melody was weak. Inspired by what she had just heard, Brown suggested that Childers ask Brooks to try his hand at writing a better melody. When the showcase was over, the three went to Brown's house at 1230 Greenfield Avenue to work on the song. After tinkering with it for a while, Brooks sang it into the four-track recorder Brown used to make demos. Then they listened to the playback.

"Ma'am, is that all right?" Brooks asked. Brown suggested he do it again "with feeling." That was all the prodding Brooks needed. He made a second run-through and, says Brown, "he just nailed it."

That weekend, Brown listened and relistened to Brooks's tape as she drove from Nashville to a second home she maintains in Alabama. "I thought, 'This kid is phenomenal. [He's] the best singer I think I've ever heard.'" When Brown came back to Nashville, she called Brooks and told him how impressed she was.

Brown also volunteered to help him search for a house to rent—one that would be big enough for him, Sandy, and the members of Santa Fe, his band from Oklahoma. Finally, Brooks located a five-bedroom house in Hendersonville, just north of Nashville, and the Sooners started moving in. Before long, the house sheltered seven adults and an eighteen-month-old child.

Throughout 1987 Randy Travis was the biggest dog in the country music kennel. All his singles that year—"Forever and Ever, Amen," "I Won't Need You Anymore," and "Too Gone Too Long"—went No. 1. In July the Country Music Association announced that that soft-spoken North Carolinian had been nominated for five of its awards: entertainer, male vocalist, single, song, and album of the year. (He would win in all but the entertainer category.) But even more impressive than the acclaim was Travis's ability to sell albums like a pop star. His first two sold more than a million copies each. And the second one, *Always & Forever*, was certi-

48

fied platinum within ten weeks of its release.

Also making noise and earning multiple CMA nominations that year were George Strait, Reba McEntire, the O'Kanes, Hank Williams, Jr. (who would beat out Travis for the top entertainer prize), George Jones, Holly Dunn, the Judds, Kathy Mattea, and Restless Heart. This was the artistic opposition Brooks faced from his crowded home in Hendersonville.

"I spent a great amount of time with Garth," Stephanie Brown says. "I've been a teacher. And when there's a young one like that who is *so* good, you're willing to give your time." From the first time she saw him perform, Brown says she was struck by his intelligence: "I thought, Here's the smartest young man I've seen. I don't want to sound like I'm belittling his talent—I don't mean that at all—but he's *so* good at PR. I've never met anybody who had as clear a grasp of what he had to do to get an audience or move through a meeting."

Realizing that Brooks needed to make contacts within Nashville's tightly woven music community, Brown took him to meet Bob Doyle, then director of member relations for ASCAP. Ironically, it was the discouraging words of another ASCAP official that had sent Brooks scurrying back to Oklahoma from Nashville two years earlier.

Doyle and Brooks, however, took an instant liking to each other. "Everbody talks like Garth came to town and I introduced him to Bob the next day," Brown says.

"It wasn't quite that quick—although it was within the first month or so."

Before Bob Doyle came to ASCAP, he had worked in the A & R (artist & repertoire) department at Warner Bros. Records, a job that required him to listen to songs and determine which ones were best for certain Warner artists. During his tenure at ASCAP, he became increasingly taken with the idea of starting his own music publishing company. In Brooks he recognized a songwriter who could some day be valuable to a publisher.

Stephanie Brown was also in the process of starting her own publishing company at this time. But she says she was too new in the business to service a writing talent like Brooks. She did advise him, though, on what to look for in a publisher and alerted him to who did and didn't have a good name in the music business.

After about six months of living in Hendersonville, Garth and Sandy moved into a tiny three-room apartment in Brown's Greenfield Avenue house. After a record deal failed to materialize, the band members who had shared the couple's earlier quarters went their own ways, most returning to Oklahoma. Brown lived upstairs, in the rooms where she now has her publishing company, and the Brookses lived on the ground floor. They stayed there for over a year, and Brooks and Brown continued to write together.

One of the jobs Brooks took after moving to Nashville was managing the Cowtown Boots store in nearby Madison.

Since he had sold athletic shoes and equipment at DuPree's in Stillwater, Brooks came to the new post with some experience. He also came with a plan. "Garth is so smart," Brown reiterates. "He got the job, became manager, and then hired Sandy. That way, you know, she could cover for him, and he could sort of take off when he needed to go to meetings."

Convenient though it was, the Cowtown job paid little—as did the string of temporary clerical jobs Sandy worked on the side. Brown says the lack of money sometimes depressed Brooks, especially if Sandy suffered. "The first awards show they went to," Brown says, "Sandy borrowed a jacket from me, and Garth didn't like that. He didn't like it because this was his wife and here she is, having to borrow clothes. It was a real touchy thing. He made more money before he came to Nashville."

Brooks told a *Time* reporter that he once became so frustrated at his lack of progress in Nashville that he parked his car and started beating himself on the head as hard as he could. "I had snapped," he admitted. "Sandy [was] screaming at me to quit. I was crying, she was crying."

Although it took Brooks less than a year to get a record contract after he moved to Nashville, that questing period was filled with disappointments, indecisions, and the impulse to go back home where he was known and respected and where the psychological territory was mapped and safe.

Sandy Brooks gave her husband the pep talks he

needed to stay on. "I knew his feelings and his love for the music was so great," Sandy told a reporter. "He just got in a rut and was ready to run from it again. I said, 'Look, I can't spend my life going back and forth, back and forth. We're here. Let's give it at least three years. If nothing happens, we'll go back.'"

Even when he seemed to be standing still, Brooks was making contacts that would soon be useful. Within those first few months, he met the producer, picker, and former label executive Jerry Kennedy, the songwriters Austin Gardner and Kent Blazy, and the singers Danielle Alexander, Joe Diffie, Billy Dean, and Trisha Yearwood. None of the singers had a recording contract at the time, but they were all making names for themselves as versatile demo singers. Kennedy, who has produced all the Statler Brothers albums since 1970, was so taken by Brooks's singing that he persuaded the powerful Buddy Lee Attractions booking agency to represent him—even before Brooks's record deal came through.

It would not be widely heard until it was released on Brooks's *Ropin' the Wind* album in 1991, but one of the songs he co-wrote with Stephanie Brown during this early period was "Burnin' Bridges." Brown says she was initially put off by the triteness of the title and theme and had to be tricked into working on it. "When he brought me the idea and wanted me to write with him, I said no," Brown remembers. "I told him it was a cliché, that there was another song by that title, and that there wasn't anything more you could say about it."

PLATINUM COWBOY 51

GARTH BROOKS 52

Brooks persisted, and Brown resisted. She pointed out that they had already written a tune called "Smoldering Ashes" and that it had about as many fire images as she could tolerate. Nonetheless, Brooks returned in a few days. "It was so typical of how Garth handles things," Brown says. "He said, 'Now, I know you're not going to write this song with me, but would you listen to my opening line?' And he sang, 'Yesterday she thanked me for oilin' that front door/This morning when she wakes up she won't be thankful anymore.' I said, 'Let's *do* write the song.'"

Austin Gardner, another of Brooks's co-writers during this period, recalls that the earnest young Oklahoman always wrote with the listener in mind: "He wanted to make sure that whatever we wrote people could dance to. That was really important to him at that time. I remember us writing one of these real tender love songs. When we got it done, we recorded it. Later, he dropped by the office and I asked him how he felt about the song—if he'd listened to the tape and all that stuff. He said, 'Man, Sandy and I danced to it.' I said, 'Did it pass the wife test?' And he said, 'Oh, yeah, it passed.' They used to love to dance. They would dance right there in their house."

Brooks had a penchant for being dramatic even when he was writing, according to Gardner. "I would throw out an idea, and he would be quiet. Real quiet. Then he would get up and start pacing around the room. He would take his hat off and put it on again. Then he would sit back down. He'd look at me, and I'd go, 'Well?' And he'd say, 'That'll work.'"

If Brooks was dramatic when he wrote, he could be downright mystical when he recorded his demos. Gardner recalls the morning Brooks came to his studio to record a "moonlight/midnight/I-worship-you type of song." The first order of business, Gardner says, was to establish the right mood. Gardner ordered all the lights turned off where Brooks was standing except for the one on his music stand. Then Brooks began to sing.

"I had only heard him sing the song in my office," Gardner says, "but here it was spiritual, he was so intense. He sang it one time through, and I remember turning to the engineer and saying that I sure hoped the tape was running. When Garth got to the end of the song, me and a couple of engineers were ready to cry. Everybody was afraid to breathe. I said, 'Man, that was perfect. Let's not change a thing. I'm in here drying my eyes. Do you want to come in and listen to it?' And he said, 'No. I can do better. Erase it and let's do it again.'

"It's a real shame that everybody around the world that loves Garth's music—his albums and his live performances—can never get that intimate experience of being with him in the studio. You know how they call these people 'recording artists'? Well, a lot of them have record deals and they're good singers. But Garth is an artist."

Songwriter Kent Blazy saw many of the same things in Brooks that Gardner did. Bob Doyle asked the more experienced Blazy to write with Brooks and teach him the essentials. The pairing eventually led to Brooks's first No. 1 song, "If Tomorrow Never Comes."

According to Blazy, Brooks came up with the idea. "He's got a better instinct and vision than just about anybody I've come across," Blazy says. "And he had that before he had a record deal. He was just very secure in who he was and what he was trying to do. When we wrote 'If Tomorrow Never Comes,' the man was probably only twenty-five years old. He had a depth and wisdom far beyond his years."

In addition to co-writing with Brooks, Blazy used him to sing demos: "The more I used him, the more I came to realize that there was nothing this man couldn't sing. Nothing threw him."

Lean and boyish Bob Doyle bowed out of his job at ASCAP in February 1988 to create Major Bob Music. One of the first two writers Doyle signed to his company was Larry Bastian, whose songs had been recorded by Eddy Arnold, Sammi Smith, and David Frizzell. The other was Garth Brooks. Then, not long after he set his publishing operation in motion, Doyle and a publicist, Pam Lewis, formed Doyle/Lewis Management. Brooks was one of its first clients.

A graduate of Wells College and later a publicist for the Warner Amex Satellite Entertainment Corporation in New York, Pam Lewis had come to Nashville in 1984 to handle media relations for RCA Records. She was by all accounts a diligent and devoted worker for the label. But her abrasiveness earned her enemies both within and without the company, and she was fired from the job less than a year after taking it.

Devastated, Lewis returned to New York to look for work, but she could find nothing. She quickly came back to Nashville and set up her own publicity company. For months, she subsisted on the accounts of nickel-and-dime clients. Then Doyle invited her to lunch and pitched the idea of the two of them forming a management company.

Years later, Lewis explained to a reporter for *Amusement Business* how single-minded she became in helping to launch Brooks's career: "Garth has a way of making people believe in his dream. I mean, I became so immersed in breaking him that I would actually dream about him at night, up there onstage accepting awards. We'd sit around and visualize, brainstorm. People would call me at work and say, 'What's up?' and I'd say, 'I've been Garthing.'"

Under Doyle's guidance, Brooks began pitching himself to every major record label in town. None showed much interest. In March Doyle contacted Jim Foglesong, head of Capitol Records' Nashville division, and asked him if he would be willing to let Brooks stop by his office for a brief, informal audition. Normally, such a request would be denied on the spot. But Foglesong knew Doyle was legitimate and that he could spot talent.

Moreover, Foglesong had nothing to lose in making the effort. At that time Capitol was laboring in the shadow of the vastly more profitable Nashville divisions of RCA, CBS, MCA, and Warner Bros. It wasn't that Capitol lacked artists. After all, the label could boast Tanya

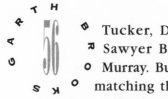

Tucker, Dan Seals, T. Graham Brown, Sawyer Brown, and the ageless Anne Murray. But none of them came close to matching the album sales of such acts as Randy Travis, George Strait, Alabama, the Judds, Reba McEntire, and Hank Williams, Jr.

Foglesong checked his calendar and told Doyle he could bring Brooks to his office on April 4.

CHAPTER FIVE

FROM THE DEAL TO THE ROAD

Brooks was "extremely ner-

vous" the day he auditioned for

Capitol, says Lynn Shults, who

recalls how the "beads of sweat"

collected on the singer's face as

he performed. Shults, who now

works for *Billboard,* was then in

charge of finding acts for Capitol.

Brooks had every reason to be

58

nervous. By this time he had pitched himself to every other record company in
town, all of which had turned him down.
This looked like his last chance.

Shults says Brooks played five or six songs
that day. But none of the Capitol staff Foglesong had
invited in to listen seemed impressed. After a round of
handshakes and the attendant perfunctory remarks,
Doyle and Brooks took their leave. Shults returned to
his office without discussing the audition with
Foglesong. "Nothing more was really thought about it
or mentioned," Shults says. "It was some time later that
the famous night at the Bluebird Cafe happened."

There is nothing remarkable about the Bluebird
Cafe beyond the fact that it was (and still is) the most
important music showcase club in Nashville. Over the
years, it had become a favorite place for songwriters
and singers, both new and established, to try out their
material on one another. Consequently, the club regularly attracted producers, publishers, and record label
talent scouts who hoped to discover the Next Big
Thing. Located in a strip mall in the Green Hills section
of town, the Bluebird has the additional advantage of
being a five-minute drive from Music Row, where most
of the labels are headquartered.

Although the Bluebird's owner, Amy Kurland, and
her staff usually decide who will perform at the
club, they sometimes let music groups stage their
own showcases there. It was through one such group,
the Nashville Entertainment Association, that Garth
Brooks made his Bluebird apprearance. That night—
May 11, 1988—Shults was in the audience.

There are several stories about the circumstances that led to Brooks being at the Bluebird that night. As Shults tells it, Ralph Murphy, a more prominent singer and songwriter, was originally scheduled to perform but failed to show up. So Brooks took his place.

Not so, says Austin Gardner, who wrote songs with Brooks in the days before he was discovered. He says Brooks had to compete for the right to perform. Gardner headed the NEA committee that listened to the audition tapes publishers and songwriters submitted in an effort to earn a spot on the shows.

To avoid any charge of favoritism, the committee required that the tapes be submitted without labels that identified the singer or songwriter (often one and the same). "Garth went through that regular motion like everybody else," Gardner asserts. "He qualified on the strength of the song and his voice."

Brooks confirms that he had been invited to perform. But he adds that "the guy who was supposed to go on second wasn't there, and the producer asked me to go on in his place."

Since he had heard Brooks before, the convivial Shults was not really all that attentive when the young singer stepped onto the thumbnail-size stage. "I don't remember what the first song was," Shults confesses, "but I'm pretty sure the second one was 'If Tomorrow Never Comes.' Garth just blew me away."

At that phase of his career, Shults was not a man who could be "blown away" easily. As a top label executive, he had worked closely with Kenny Rogers, Crystal Gayle, and Anne Murray when they were at the peak of their popularity. And he had fought—unsuccessfully—to have his label sign the dazzling innovative Ricky Skaggs.

"Being on the road with a lot of great artists," he says, "you get this frame of reference for what is exceptional. And that night Garth was exceptional. It was something that in no way came across in the room that day with Jim and me. This was not with a band, either. This was just Garth and an acoustic guitar. But his vocal performance and his magnetism of personality connected with people who didn't even know who Garth Brooks was. What went through my mind was that I had just seen somebody who was as good as—if not better than—anyone I had ever seen."

With that thought in mind, Shults says he decided he had better offer to sign Brooks before another label did: "Immediately after he finished, I went over to Bob Doyle, who was standing by the bar, and I said, 'You guys got a deal, and as far as I'm concerned, it's an album deal.' [The more cautious singles deal, which was then common in Nashville, committed a label only to releasing one or more singles on an artist.] We made a handshake agreement. The next morning I went into Jim's office, and I told him what had happened and what I had done. He asked me if I absolutely believed in Garth this much. I told him I never felt stronger about anything in my life. And he said okay."

In recounting the Bluebird incident, Brooks told the writer Alanna Nash: "I'll never forget [Lynn Shults] for being not only a big enough man but [also] professional enough to say, 'Maybe we missed something. Why don't you come in.'"

By Gardner's account, the crowd was fairly subdued when Brooks ended his set: "It wasn't like everybody stood up and cheered. You've got to remember
that the only people in the club were music industry
executives and other songwriters. There were no ordinary fans in the room. The applause was real strong,
but at the same time it was like you could hear brain
cells clicking together—because you had like three or
four heads of different labels, eight different producers, and five A & R people in the room. Nobody wanted to jump up on their chairs and start screaming
because somebody else might sign him."

Capitol officially signed Brooks on June 17 and
reportedly gave him a modest ten-thousand-dollar
advance. Shults was immediately faced with the job of
finding him the right producer. Artistically, this selection is a life or death matter, since producers aren't all
equal in their ability to hear and nourish the special talents of each new artist. "I started listening to his demo
tapes," Shults says, "and I realized that this was an artist
who had many elements and components—everything
from the James Taylor kind of material to music with a
rock edge. I knew we had to make sure he was
matched up with a producer who could see the big
picture and get musically in sync with him."

In conjunction with Brooks's managers, Shults
put together a list of possible producers and sent the
singer out to "interview" them. "You don't
just turn somebody over to a producer,"
Shults maintains. "The artist and the producer have got to spend time talking
together about music and a lot of other

issues." Ultimately, Brooks said he was inclined toward Allen Reynolds. That suited Shults, who had worked with Reynolds at Jack Clement's short-lived JMI label. Later, he had matched Crystal Gayle with Reynolds, who went on to produce her top hits. "I just knew he was a guy who could stretch more musically than most producers in this town," Shults adds. At the time, Reynolds was also producing Kathy Mattea.

Because both men were well versed in rock, pop, and blues, as well as country, Memphis-born Reynolds was the ideal choice to record Brooks. Starting out as a singer and songwriter, Reynolds had recorded for a number of small labels during the 1960s and 1970s. His song "Five O'Clock World" was a Top 5 hit for the Vogues in 1966. (The same song was a recent country hit for Hal Ketchum, who Reynolds also produces.) In 1978 Reynolds was himself on the country charts briefly with "Wrong Road Again," one of his own compositions that had earlier been a hit for Crystal Gayle. A less sensitive or more musically limited producer would certainly have stifled or discouraged Capitol's new hope.

While Brooks was in the studio with Reynolds that summer and fall, working on his album, the Capitol team was putting together plans to launch his career as a recording artist. In addition to Foglesong and Shults, the label crew included Paul Lovelace in radio promotion, Gerrie McDowell in sales, and Bonnie Rasmussen (now Taggert) in publicity. Doyle and Lewis were also deeply involved in the strategy meetings, as was Joe

Harris, Brooks's booking agent at Buddy Lee Attractions.

It is a long and an enormously complex process from first signing to album release—particularly when a record label is turning out dozens of different albums a year. For his part, Brooks had to write and select songs for his album, record them, pose for publicity and album cover photos, do interviews, call and visit radio stations to butter up the people who would (or wouldn't) program his music, and put together and rehearse a band. While that was going on, various people at the label were designing an overall marketing plan for the album, creating a budget, turning out press kits, determining the kind of "image" Brooks should project, selecting a title for the album, designing the album cover, selecting which of the songs should be released as singles, estimating the number of albums to be manufactured, staging showcases for the press and record retailers, scheduling press and radio tours, sending out advance copies of the album to reviewers, and deciding when the album should be released to record stores.

More than ten months elapsed between the time Brooks signed with Capitol and the time his first single was released. And it was an additional month before his first album made its debut.

Instead of waiting for radio airplay alone to introduce Brooks to American listeners, the Capitol team persuaded him to start touring—hoping that his live concerts would make key markets more eager for his records. Capitol also budgeted money for three music videos from the album.

Shults estimates that Capitol set aside $300,000 for tour support shortfall. This didn't mean that the label would actually have to spend that much. Rather, it was funds reserved to cover any difference between what it actually cost to keep Brooks and his band on the road and what the band would take in through ticket sales. With the album itself budgeted at around $100,000 and three proposed music videos totaling the same amount, Capitol was making a half-million dollar bet on the kid from Yukon.

Tim Bowers, who was Brooks's road manager and bass player for two years, says that Brooks started recruiting band members as soon as his Capitol deal was confirmed. Bowers joined the new band in September 1988, although he says the serious touring didn't get underway until the following May, just after the album came out. Not long after he met Brooks, Bowers went to see him perform solo at one of Stephanie Brown's "Circle of Friends" showcases. Brooks had to follow what Bowers describes as "an extremely good rockabilly band" that had gotten the crowd "really jazzed and carrying on." Brooks walked onstage and began singing. "I watched him—in half a song—quiet the whole room," Bowers says, "to where all eyes were focused on him."

The songwriter Alice Randall, a friend of Bob Doyle's, remembers how valiantly Brooks and his band rehearsed to get ready for the road: "He used to practice down in the basement [of Doyle's office] with his band. That basement was a horror—dingy, dirty, unfinished, a dirt floor—or at least a floor covered with dirt. I used to sit at the top of the stairs and listen to them. That's where I heard him sing 'Mr. Blue' the first time. But what impressed me was his complete discipline to be able to go down there and rehearse." Another thing Randall recalls is that Doyle was even then predicting that Brooks was going to be "as big as Elvis."

After many a meeting and much discussion, Capitol's marketing and promotion people concluded that they would release "Much Too Young (to Feel This Damn Old)" as Brooks's first single. It was not a terribly original song. In fact, it sounded comfortingly familiar. There were a thousand other country songs about road-weariness, and many of them had become classics. Some, such as "King of the Road," were about hoboes. Others, like "Six Days on the Road" and "Drivin' My Life Away," centered on the ordeals of truck drivers. Larry Gatlin's "Houston (Means I'm One Day Closer to You)" was one of several laments from the viewpoint of touring country singers. But "Much Too Young" has even a closer ancestor. In its detailing of a battered rodeo rider's life, it sounded very much like George Strait's 1983 hit "Amarillo by Morning." Since Brooks credits Strait with giving him an artistic focus in 1981, it's understandable that there would be echoes of "Amarillo" in the newer song. One could do much worse, the Capitolists no doubt thought, than conjure up memories of the best-selling Strait.

Billboard gave Brooks's single a so-so review in its March 4 issue, calling it "a dark but up-tempo essay on the rigors of road-weariness and loneliness." The review lauded Brooks's "spirited, cry-in-the-voice" interpretation and the record's "moody, imaginative instrumentation." Clearly, the reviewer was not overwrought with enthusiasm.

History is seldom as dramatic as it should have been. The one-man cavalry who had ridden in from Oklahoma to save country music did not arrive on the charts at a gallop. At best, it was a slow trot. "Much Too Young" edged into *Billboard*'s Hot Country Singles chart on March 25, 1989, at a barely visible No. 94. It ranked well behind such other new singles as Roseanne Cash's "I Don't Want to Spoil the Party," Larry Boone's "Wine Me Up," and James House's "Don't Quit Me Now."

If there was a good omen on the chart for Brooks that week, it was that Reba McEntire, a fellow Oklahoman, occupied the No. 1 spot with her ballad "New Fool at an Old Game." Clint Black, whose success would soon become the standard by which Brooks measured his own, was at No. 35 that week and moving up fast with his first single, "A Better Man." For the next several months Brooks would continue to look at the young Texan's back.

At that time, country music was in good if not radiant health. The "new traditionalists"—Randy Travis, Dwight Yoakam, Ricky Van Shelton, and Keith Whitley—were creating some excitement, and the top names were regularly racking up album sales of a million or more each. K. T. Oslin had emerged from nowhere to give Reba McEntire a run for her money. And the Judds and Alabama were almost as popular as they had been in the early 1980s. In other words, Brooks wasn't exactly riding into a wasteland. Still, older acts were commanding a large share of the charts. Of the one hundred singles listed that week, forty-six were by acts that had been recording since the 1970s or earlier. Most of them were excellent performers, but they tended to attract older listeners who did not buy many records.

While Brooks was getting his band up and running, Capitol was planning a tour that would target locations in the Southeast and Southwest, traditionally the most receptive markets for country music. On the tour he would play small clubs, visit record retailers, glad-hand the DJs at country radio stations along the way, and otherwise attempt to spread the good news that he had arrived. By the time "Much Too Young (to Feel This Damn Old)" was released, he was, according to Shults, "almost living in Dallas." The label figured that a big hit in a market that large would have national reverberations. Shults says there was some concern over whether the notoriously conservative country radio stations would play a song with "damn" in the title, but most of them did.

From the start it was evident that Brooks wanted to be a star as much as Capitol wanted to make him one. Even at the tiny clubs where virtually no one showed up, he worked as hard as if he were playing a stadium. Bonnie Taggert, who headed Capitol's publicity depart-

PLATINUM COWBOY 67

ment, went with Brooks on a swing through Raleigh, North Carolina. His schedule called for him to make a courtesy call at a record chain headquarters, be the guest of honor at the grand opening of a Wal-Mart, and then perform a full show that evening at a local nightclub. (It is the kind of scorched-earth regimen most new acts have to endure at first—or else.)

"This was the first time I'd seen his performance," Taggert says. "He was captivating. He had everybody in that room going. He did 'Friends in Low Places,' and by the second chorus, all the people were standing up front where the dance floor was and singing along. Garth has this way of just reaching out and putting people in the palm of his hands and holding them throughout the performance." Some of the people in the audience, Taggert explains, had come to see the then much more famous Delbert McClinton, who was playing the room next door. But she says they waited until Brooks was finished before flocking to McClinton's show.

Taggert had only one mild complaint about working with Brooks during those debut months: He was just too courteous. "He was *so* polite. I always felt so old because he always called me 'ma'am.' I grew up in California, and you don't say 'ma'am' to anybody. But with him, everything was 'Yes, ma'am' and 'No, ma'am.' I just wanted to slap him."

On April 12 Capitol released Brooks's self-titled album. To announce its arrival, the label bought a full-page ad in *Billboard*. The ad carried a picture of the album cover and a larger full-length photo of Brooks standing in the woods, gazing contemplatively to the right, his hands crossed and resting on his guitar. Headlined "A Capitol Country Commitment," the ad proclaims, "When an artist delivers a debut album with the outstanding material and superb vocals that one would only expect from a veteran, you release it with pride... and a firm commitment." Illustrating the tentative nature of selecting singles, the ad cites four songs by name: "Much Too Young," "If Tomorrow Never Comes" "Nobody Gets Off in This Town," and "Cowboy Bill." The implication was that these four were the most likely singles. As it turns out, the last two names never made it to single status. Instead, "Not Counting You" and "The Dance" were chosen in their place.

"Brooks invests this debut album with immense charm, sensitivity and vocal authority," said the *Billboard* review. *USA Today* also gave the project a good play, running a picture of Brooks and applauding his "heartfelt, hurtin' vocals and country timelessness."

Just as Brooks's star was rising, another's fell to earth.

On May 9 a radio news bulletin sent a chill through the sunny Nashville afternoon: Keith Whitley was dead. Reports said that the thirty-three-year-old singer had drunk himself to death in one marathon binge at his home that morning. His widow, Lorrie Morgan, was notified while she was en route to a show in Alaska. The tragedy was compounded by several circumstances. Since the release of his immensely popular album *Don't Close Your Eyes* the year before,

Whitley's star had been steadily rising. Moreover, he and Morgan, his second wife, had recently had their first baby. But the most agonizing element was the surprise of it all. Even those close to Whitley believed he had finally beaten his long dependence on alcohol.

The country music industry had not been so shocked by the death of one of its own since Mel Street, another artist full of promise, committed suicide eleven years earlier. On the morning following Whitley's death, anonymous grievers tied black ribbons on lampposts the whole length of Music Row.

Although Brooks did not know Whitley personally, he was once again haunted by the specter of someone with so much promise dying so young. It brought to mind Jim Kelley and Heidi Miller—the two friends he had lost in college and to whose "loving memories" he had dedicated his first album.

The loving representation of Whitley in "The Dance" would show how much Brooks was moved and directed by the tragedy.

Because "Much Too Young (to Feel This Damn Old)" was such a somber song, Shults and his colleagues at Capitol thought they should follow it with something a bit lighter. Their first choice was that droll bit of village bashing called "Nobody Gets Off in This Town." The song was hummable, everybody could identify with it, and it would show people that this Brooks guy was good for a laugh. Shults credits Paul Lovelace, Capitol's vice president of promotion, with holding out for something even better: "He said, 'We've got to change records. We're into a serious album by a serious artist, and I don't think we should come with this borderline novelty record.'" At the last minute, the label pulled the plug on "Nobody Gets Off" and chose instead the song that would soon become the first of Brooks's many No. 1 singles, "If Tomorrow Never Comes." It was released in late August, a few weeks after "Much Too Young" had peaked on the charts at a very respectable No. 8.

Except for the people who had seen him perform in clubs, Brooks was still essentially an artist without a face. To correct that deficiency, Capitol decided to produce a music video of "If Tomorrow Never Comes." The video was especially poignant to Brooks, coming as it did at a time when he was preoccupied with long and exhausting tours that took him away from Sandy for weeks at a time. "So tell that someone that you love / just what you're thinking of / if tomorrow never comes," the song advises. To drive that message home, the video showed a contemplative Brooks against a backdrop of scenes involving three generations: a little girl, a young woman, and an elderly woman. The singer Steve Gatlin's daughter, Aubrey, played the young girl/daughter figure, and Sandy Brooks took the part of the young woman/wife. Each scene showed the quiet joy of being close to a loved one. The video was completed in late July.

Shults says he went with Brooks and his wife to see the video as it was going through the final editing stages at the Scene Three studios in Nashville. Brooks had just come in from the road. "It was just awesome power in that room coming off the video," Shults recounts.

72

"And Garth broke. He couldn't talk; he couldn't say anything. He walked out of the room and went over to his pickup truck and just sat by himself." Puzzled by this display of emotion, Shults turned to Sandy Brooks. "I said something to her like, 'I don't know what all this means, but I've never seen anyone respond to a video this way.' And she said, 'Well, maybe one day you'll know.'"

What Sandy Brooks did not explain to Shults was that her marriage had already begun to tear under the strain of her husband's ambition, absence, and attraction to other women.

Brooks was fighting another demon besides lust and loneliness during that breakthrough year toward stardom, and its name was Clint Black. Everywhere he turned, he heard music critics and industry insiders alike proclaiming that Black was the most exciting thing in country music. He was trouncing Brooks on the charts and selling albums like a superstar. To hear people talk, it seemed that no other new act—not Alan Jackson, not Travis Tritt, not Garth Brooks—really mattered.

To go back and reconstruct how Black and Brooks each blew out of their home states to converge on Nashville—and each other—is like having a satellite view of developing storms.

At about the time Garth and Sandy Brooks were just getting settled in Nashville and wondering if they should have ever left Oklahoma, Black was facing quite another dilemma. Then a part-time bar singer in Houston, he had written a song he thought had real possibilities, and a local music publisher had offered him $250 for it. That sounded like a lot of money to Black, who was working construction jobs for a living and whose singing was earning him virtually nothing. Still, he feared if he sold the song—which sounded to him like a potential hit—he might be letting go of the one thing that could take him out of Houston's urban cowboy dives and onto a record label. What he really needed, he decided, was some good advice. He had to find a manager.

Through an acquaintance, the twenty-five-year-old Black gained an audience with the reclusive Bill Ham, the manager for ZZ Top. After a series of meetings, during which Black showed his stuff as a singer and songwriter, Ham signed him to both a management and a publishing contract. Ham then decreed that Black take his songs to Nashville to look for a record deal. Failing that, he might at least pique the interest of a producer who would, in turn, find a label for him.

Black and his handlers came to Nashville in October 1987 and began making the rounds. The official ears at Warner Bros. Records listened, agreed that Black had talent, but ultimately concluded that the label really didn't need another male singer, what with having Randy Travis and Dwight Yoakam on board already. Kyle Lehning, one of the first megaproducers Ham's people approached, also passed on working with Black, since he was fully occupied producing Travis and Dan Seals.

The Ham contingency moved on to RCA Records. RCA had Alabama, the Judds,

74 and K. T. Oslin on the roster; but aside from Ronnie Milsap and Keith Whitley, none of the label's male singers was selling very many albums. Joe Galante, the head of RCA/Nashville at the time, personally auditioned Black. After hearing four of his songs, Galante told the young singer, "Clint, if you don't fart onstage, you've got a deal." In December, however, before the contract was actually signed, Galante and his staff flew to Houston to watch Black perform at the Backstage Bar. They had to see if he looked as good onstage as he sounded on tape. He did.

By Christmas—only seven months after he began his quest for a manager—Black found himself signed to the hottest country music label in existence. Three months later he was in the studio, working on his first album for RCA. At that point Garth Brooks was still polishing his songs, grinding out demos, doing showcases, and knocking on record company doors that were no more receptive to him than Warner Bros. had been to Black.

Black would have had a far bigger head start on Brooks had not RCA been so meticulous and deliberate in launching his career. Black completed his album in the summer of 1988, just as Brooks was coming aboard at Capitol. Although no singles had yet been released from Black's album, RCA rented a bus and, in September, took Black on a tour of radio stations and record stores. The aims were to introduce the project and find out from this select group of listeners which songs were the most "commercial." After chewing over all this data, RCA released Black's first single, "A Better Man," in early February, more than a year after Black came to the label.

Capitol acted much more quickly with Brooks. *His* first single, "Much Too Young," was shipped to radio stations less than a month after "A Better Man" made its debut. But because Black was already well known to radio programmers through his visits to them, "A Better Man" leaped onto the charts virtually the moment it left the pressing plant. It had a six-week lead on the chart and reached the No. 1 slot on June 10, when "Much Too Young" was chugging along at No. 23.

It was really at this point—when both artists were first achieving visibility and critical notice—that the rivalry between Black and Brooks started brewing. In rising to No. 1 on the country charts, "A Better Man" became the first debut single to reach that position since Jessi Colter's "I'm Not Lisa" achieved the same in 1975. By September, Black's album, *Killin' Time,* had been certified gold, and by February 1990 it had reached platinum. Black was the talk—and some said the hope—of the country music business.

According to Lynn Shults, Brooks's managers, Bob Doyle and Pam Lewis, were obsessed with the fear that Black would continue to eclipse their client. "It was like, 'We've got to do this and we've got to do that because Clint Black is doing this and that,'" Shults says. "Well, I knew I couldn't tell them then—and I'm hesitant to say it now— but there was no way way we could go in at that moment and compete with Clint Black."

The problem in going head-to-head with Black, as Shults saw it, was simply that Capitol couldn't match RCA's artist development team, nor could Doyle and Lewis match Bill Ham's clout. Shults was convinced that Brooks sang and wrote better than Black and that he was an infinitely more gifted stage performer. Still, Shults thought it would take a while to build Brooks's momentum.

Doyle and Lewis weren't the only ones who had Black on the brain. Brooks was preoccupied as well. To a former athlete like Brooks, Black represented something far more menacing than the opposing team. "He was the guy who was stealing all the sunshine—all the light," Brooks says. He was standing in Black's shadow and "screaming at the top of my voice, but no one could hear me because of all the noise they were making [over Clint]."

When "If Tomorrow Never Comes" went No. 1 in September 1989, Brooks thereby served notice that he aimed to play in Black's league. While Doyle and Lewis didn't have Bill Ham's muscle, they did know how to make the most of every break. During that period, The Nashville Network was planning to test a police adventure series that would be set in Nashville. It would be called "Nashville Beat" and star the buddy-team from the old "Adam 12" series, Kent McCord and Martin Milner. Brooks's managers were able to get him a job entertaining the cast filming the pilot. That led to an on-camera appearance, in which Brooks portrays himself as a club singer and sings "The Dance." The pilot aired October 21 but failed to gain high enough ratings to merit a series.

Both Garth and Sandy Brooks have recounted in interviews the long-distance phone clash that turned their marriage around—just when it was about to crash and burn. Garth had been on tour the last six months of 1989, during which time, according to Sandy, she had been with her husband only twenty-eight days. That separation alone would have been enough to spark resentment. But worse still were the reports filtering back to Sandy that Garth was cheating on her. Whether his straying was isolated or habitual, Garth has not specified, but it was sufficient for Sandy to issue an ultimatum. On November 4, she phoned him in Sikeston, Missouri, and told him that her bags were packed and her plane ticket bought. He would either come home and resolve the problem to her satisfaction or she would leave him. It was that simple.

Brooks admits that the prospect of losing the woman who had helped him keep his dreams alive devastated him. Before he could return to Nashville, though, he had to play a concert the next night in Cape Girardeau, Missouri, where he was opening for Eddie Rabbitt and Kenny Rogers. Numbed by guilt and dread, it took everything he had to face the crowd that evening.

Here's how Peter Kinder, who reviewed the concert for the *Southeast Missourian*, saw Brooks's torment—and resilience:

> This relative newcomer to stardom strode out and played for 20

minutes, managing to establish rather a good rapport with the audience, most of whom had come to see the other two per-formers. He was able to accomplish this despite a persistent hoarseness, especially evident in his speaking voice.

Brooks opened with "We Bury The Hatchet But Leave The Handle Stickin' Out," which was followed by his current hit with its amusing lyrics, "I'm Much Too Young To Feel This Damn Old" [*sic*].

Brooks exhibited another, far more debilitating problem as he seemed near tears, overcome by a never-explained emo-tional malady. This became particularly acute as Brooks launched into that heart-tugging ballad of love for the lady in his life, "If Tomorrow Never Comes." Some 45 seconds into the song, Brooks startled the crowd by stopping his band, falling silent, and then speaking of the "hell" of being on the road, of his love for the woman back home, and how some "bad things are going on." This was as specific as he got. Upon regaining composure, he asked of an empathetic and appreciative crowd, "Could I try again?" and proceeded through a workmanlike version that the crowd loved.

After two more songs, Brooks departed to a standing ovation from half the crowd, telling a puzzled audience that he hoped they might see him on another evening, one that was "not so sad."

Even from this distance in time, Brooks's emotional agony is almost palpable. It seems clear that by opening with the raucous "We Bury the Hatchet," itself a tale of domestic squabbling, Brooks was trying not just to stir up the crowd but also to soothe the sting of his own wounds. But the most remarkable element in this tableau was his masterful showmanship—his ability to turn real grief into real triumph.

A NEW
TEAM
AND A
NEW
SUPER-
STAR

CHAPTER SIX

Two weeks before Christmas
1989, the entire staff of Capitol
Records' Nashville operations was
fired. The man who wielded the
axe was the industry gadfly Jimmy
Bowen. For Jim Foglesong, it was
déjà vu of the most painful sort.
Five years earlier, Bowen had
bumped him out of the presidency

of MCA Records/Nashville. It was a rewind experience for publicist Bonnie Taggert, too. Bowen had fired her earlier from Warner Bros. Now he was at it again. The affable Lynn Shults was affably told that his services were no longer required. Within hours the only familiar face at Capitol was the receptionist, and she left within a week.

During the year and a half before he took over Capitol, Bowen had headed his own country label, Universal Records. In September he had publicly denied the rumors that Universal was in trouble, even though none of its artists at the time were selling significant numbers of records.

With his move to Capitol Bowen had, in a period of ten years, seized the helms of five major country record companies, always ruffling feathers or worse at each new stop. A brilliant speaker, tireless producer, and relentless self-promoter, Bowen's every step caused waves. It wasn't just that he replaced executives and dropped artists when he came to a label, he also had a habit of appointing himself co-producer of most of the acts—particularly the high-profile ones—on the labels he headed. Some acts, convinced that Bowen had the magic touch, dropped their former producers and asked him to produce them. Thus had Bowen become the studio mentor for such gold and platinum artists as Reba McEntire, the Oak Ridge Boys, George Strait, Hank Williams, Jr., and Conway Twitty.

The new kid at Capitol, Garth Brooks, had sold 250,000 albums within the past seven months, making him, by that label's standards, very high profile indeed. Many predicted that Allen Reynolds's days as Brooks's producer were numbered.

Bowen told reporters, however, that he intended to exercise a hands-off policy toward existing artist-producer relationships: "I have never walked into any label and said to any artist, 'You have to quit working with producer so-and-so and come work with me.' Why would you mess with anything that's working?"

Whether the new management at Capitol Records made Garth Brooks a big star or whether Brooks made Capitol a big country label is a question that will be debated around Music Row campfires for years to come. It is documentably clear, though, that the Bowen era has been enormously profitable for both parties. In spite of his strong sense of loyalty to people who helped him along the way, Brooks seems convinced that the old regime wasn't bold enough to achieve what the new one ultimately did. "I loved that first family," Brooks told Alanna Nash, "and I agree with some of their tactics. But the truth is, Bowen knows his shit about putting records out." Brooks's complaint was that the former management didn't get enough of his records into the stores to entice people to buy them.

In spite of the massive shakeup at his home label, Brooks had little spare time during the spring of 1990 to worry about label politics. He was booked to tour the West Coast with Holly Dunn and open a series of fair shows for Reba McEntire. He had to make an appearance at the Country Radio Seminar in March and play the Farm Aid benefit in early April. And there was also the matter of scheduling a few days to shoot another video. This one would be on "The Dance."

Each year, in late February or early March, thousands of disc jockeys and program directors swarm to the sprawling Opryland Hotel in Nashville for the Country Radio Seminar. It is a vital event for artists, primarily because it enables them to meet—and flatter— the people who decide if and how often their records will be played. The high point of the festivities each year is the "New Faces Show" on the last night of the seminar. It showcases ten acts who have already gained some recognition but who are still new faces to most DJs.

By the time the 1990 seminar opened, Brooks had one popular video and one No. 1 single to his credit, and his third single, "Not Counting You," was flying up the charts. Besides, he was beginning to sell albums like an established act. Clint Black was doing even better. Neither quite fit the New Faces mold, and neither was picked for the show.

But Brooks knew it was important for the programmers to see what his live performance was like. He had converted more than one skeptic and fence-sitter this way. His managers succeeded in getting him a slot at the March 2 luncheon that ASCAP was throwing for the conventioneers. Brooks would perform on a bill with Alan Jackson and the now-defunct group Billy Hill. Radio people are notoriously hard to dazzle, particularly at something as stiff and formal as a luncheon. Brooks knew precisely what to do to fix that. When his turn came, he swung into a manic rendition of "Friends in Low Places," a song from his upcoming album, and made believers out of everyone there. From that point on, few in country radio wondered if Brooks had "staying power."

To promote Brooks as a concert act while the year's booking season was still young, his managers, label, and booking agency placed a full-page ad in *Billboard,* announcing that "Garth Brooks & Stillwater" was ready to rock. "Bring 'em to your town," the ad trumpeted, "and watch 'em burn it down." Across the photo of Brooks and his six band members was boldly stamped "Sold Out." That was wishful thinking in those days but utterly true in the years to come.

During this same period, the increasingly busy and prosperous Brooks hired his brother Kelly as tour accountant and his sister Betsy as harmony singer. In time, they would take over all the duties Brooks had originally employed Tim Bowers to do.

Brooks was one of the zillion or so performers who responded to Willie Nelson's call for talent for the Farm Aid IV concert on April 7 in Indianapolis. Indeed, there were so many acts wedged into the fourteen-hour-long show at the Hoosier Dome that few had the opportunity to shine. He was wedged onto a bill with such heavyweights as Nelson, John Mellencamp, Guns N' Roses, Bonnie Raitt, Bill Monroe, John Denver, Carl Perkins, Crosby, Stills & Nash, and John Prine. At

GARTH BROOKS

At this point in his career, Brooks's brief appearance drew about the same polite applause as was accorded fellow "hat acts" Alan Jackson and Ricky Van Shelton.

While the mood of the day was generally festive, there was one very dark thread running through it. In a hospital a few blocks away from the stadium, eighteen-year-old Ryan White lay dying of AIDS. The boy had been infected by a transfusion, and his good-humored efforts to make people more understanding of the disease had earned him respect and headlines around the world. Michael Jackson had sought him out, and the two had become friends. Other celebrities made a point of keeping in touch with White and speaking of his personal bravery. But finally the disease overwhelmed him. Nelson, Kris Kristofferson, and the Reverend Jesse Jackson slipped away from the concert in progress to stand at White's bedside.

Inside the stadium, rumor was spreading that a "surprise musical guest" would close the show. Some speculated it would be Paul McCartney. Others thought it might be Bob Dylan. But just after midnight, as the evening neared its end, it was a subdued Elton John who came onstage. He had been with Ryan White for the last several hours and had reluctantly left him to make this appearance. In the most moving moment of an emotionally supercharged day, John touched the keys of his piano and said to the crowd, "This one's for Ryan." Then he sang "Candle in the Wind."

Ryan White died later that morning.

Shortly before his 1992 tour, Brooks would tell interviewers that he wanted to learn to play the piano so he could do "Candle in the Wind" in his shows. And surely White's story was in his thoughts when he paid tribute to others who had died before their time in "The Dance."

In late April 1990 Brooks was in California to play a concert and prepare for the Academy of Country Music's awards show. He was nominated for three awards—best new male vocalist and song and single record of the year (both for "If Tomorrow Never Comes"). The show was being broadcast live from the Pantages Theater in Los Angeles on April 25. The evening before, Brooks finally got to meet the man he had memorialized (and publicized) in "Much Too Young (to Feel This Damn Old)"—the rodeo star turned singer Chris LeDoux. The scene of that momentous encounter was The Cocky Bull in Victorville, California, where both were booked to play. The awards ceremony was a less uplifting occasion. Clint Black, his chart adversary, beat him out for the new male vocal and single honors; and "Where've You Been" triumphed over "If Tomorrow Never Comes" for the top song award.

Without question, the music video for "The Dance" did more than anything else to transform Brooks from one of the pack to King of the Universe. Through the video, Brooks effectively announced that he wasn't just singing songs for people but also suggesting ways they should look at themselves and the world.

It is chilling to realize that Brooks almost didn't record "The Dance." Even after it was recorded, few at his label thought it should be released as a single. Had it not been, there would have been no video, and history would have taken another turn.

Brooks says he first heard the songwriter Tony Arata sing "The Dance" at the Bluebird Cafe. The Georgia-born Arata, who is a few years older than Brooks, had recorded for the Noble Vision label in the mid-1980s. But until "The Dance" made him famous, Arata was best known as the writer of the Jim Glaser hit, "The Man in the Mirror." Brooks recalls that Arata evoked only a modest response from the Bluebird crowd: "People were very polite when it was over, and the voice inside me was standing up and screaming, 'Didn't any of you hear what I heard?'"

Having heard what the others didn't, Brooks asked Arata for a demo of "The Dance" and took it to Allen Reynolds with the suggestion it be considered for the impending album. He then promptly forgot about it. Near the end of the selection process, Reynolds suggested to Brooks that he record the song. "I said, 'I don't know, Allen, if it's country enough.'" To which Reynolds firmly replied, "Trust me on this one." Happily, Brooks did.

Reynolds could have made "The Dance" sound "country" had he speeded up the tempo just a little and backed the vocal with an acoustic guitar. But the song warranted a lighter hand. To establish its moody and bittersweet tone, the pianist Bobby Wood laid down an airy, wistful introductory line, one that suggests resolution emerging from emotional confusion. The same ethereal sound delicately threads its way through the lyrics, always implying that the song holds more than its text. And at the end, the haunting piano plays on past the lyrics, like a benign spirit searching. Reynolds crafted and Brooks interpreted that rare kind of song that comes alive at first hearing.

Capitol released "The Dance" single in mid-April, a few weeks before the video was completed. The *Billboard* review proclaimed it to be "easily the most eloquently written and sensitively interpreted love song of the past decade." The video would receive even greater raves.

Brooks's concept for the video was both simple and masterful. In his mind, "The Dance" was only incidentally a love song. As he saw it, the song was primarily about risking everything for one's dream. What better way to illustrate this point than by showing a gallery of great dreamers, all of whom had paid the ultimate price—their lives—for the dreams? Deciding who best exemplified these traits was a little tricky. John F. Kennedy and Martin Luther King, Jr., were naturals. But John Wayne was more of a stretch since cancer, not dreams, had killed him. Still, his visage had become a symbol for all things heroic, and his resistance to the fatal disease was its own kind of heroism. So he would fit. Keith Whitley was still fresh in Brooks's mind and obviously an example of death arriving cruelly early. Like Icarus of legend, the crew of the doomed

Challenger spacecraft had ambitiously reached for the heavens and had tragically fallen short. He would include them as well.

All these figures—even Whitley—were widely known. The only puzzler—at least to those outside of rodeo circles—was the inclusion of Lane Frost. The video identified him by name, and the footage suggested he was a successful bull rider. But that was the extent of it. One could only conclude he had died young by assuming he shared the common denominator of the others. Given Brooks's affinity for the rodeo (and life's larger meanings), though, his choice of Frost was perfect. Frost embodied precisely the right virtues of purpose and daring. And just as Brooks was then having to do, Frost had been a young man who had to gradually come to terms with fame and money.

Frost had been killed by a bull at a rodeo in Cheyenne, Wyoming, less than a year before the video was made. He was twenty-five at the time of his death and had earned nearly half a million dollars in prize money during the previous six years. To Brooks, the parallels were obvious.

All these details aside, the part of the video that defined Brooks and gave the message an edge were his intense opening remarks. Standing in front of a bare backdrop and talking directly to the viewer, Brooks introduced the song this way: "To a lot of people, I guess 'The Dance' is a love-gone-bad song, which, you know, that it is. To me, it's always been a song about life—or maybe the loss of, those people that have given the ultimate sacrifice for a dream that they believed in, like the John F. Kennedys or the Martin Luther Kings, the John Waynes or the Keith Whitleys. And if they could come back, I think they would say to us what the lyrics of 'The Dance' say."

It may have been scripted, but the introduction had the rough, stop-and-go sound of one who is slowly picking just the right words to say something quite important.

Just after the first notes of the song begin, Brooks speaks once more: "Naturally, when we were looking for a way to do this video, this is what we came up with." The message here, of course, is, We both know this is a video, but it's really a lesson about how to live.

In the video for "If Tomorrow Never Comes," there were occasional flashes of Brooks's penetrating, mesmerizing eyes, but in "The Dance" the camera returns to them again and again. They are eyes that seem to take in and understand all that they fix themselves on.

At the end of the song, Brooks tells the viewer: "You know, I would never compare myself with the folks that are seen in the video. But if for some reason, God forbid, I should leave this world unexpectedly, I hope they play 'The Dance' for me. I mean, that's it: I could have missed the pain, but I'd have had to miss the dance. I wouldn't miss this for the world."

In just over three minutes, Brooks conveyed the image of a man who is aware, reflective, calm, focused, sympathetic, commonplace, open, tender, modest, admiring—and, yes, even "politically correct." No other country singer came even close to projecting such an alluring array of virtues. The video was a forceful declaration that country music could be as universal and profound as any other kind.

The Nashville Network began showing "The Dance" in mid-May, and Country Music Television put it in heavy play in early June. It didn't take long for the viewers to confirm the video's appeal and emotional power. One wrote CMT about breaking into tears when she first saw it. Another wrote: "I lost my husband after thirty-four years of marriage. It wasn't easy. I missed him terribly. When I saw this video, I thought, 'If I'd have missed this pain, I would have missed the dance, the thirty-four good years we had together.' And I wouldn't have missed them for the world. So, you see, it helped me accept reality. There is always a price for the good things in life. Do we not want to buy anything for fear we might lose it? I think God had more of a hand in this song than people may realize."

"The Dance" became Brooks's second No. 1 hit, and the video went on to win the Country Music Association's video of the year award.

In June Brooks made his first singing appearance at Fan Fair, the annual week-long series of concerts and autograph sessions that brings twenty-four-thousand country music die-hards to the Tennessee State Fairgrounds. Before Brooks left the stage, label chief Jimmy Bowen presented him with a gold record, signifying that 500,000 copies of *Garth Brooks* had been sold.

Brooks performed at the mammoth Jamboree in the Hills festival in July and afterward came to the press trailer to talk to reporters. He thanked those who complimented him on "The Dance" video, explained Allen Reynolds's part in the whole affair, and likened Reynolds to "a big pair of hands"—ready to guide him or catch him if he fell. When the inevitable reference to Clint Black came up, Brooks told how a fan had mistaken him for Black following the CMA Awards Show last October. He says he told her he was flattered by the comparison but that he wasn't in the same league with Black. As keenly as he felt the competition, he never passed up the chance to say good things about Black. Such displays of courtesy have endeared him to his fans.

In a matter of a few months, though, Brooks would be letting his sales figures talk for him. By late July, Clint Black's album had sold 1.6 million copies, but Brooks was coming on strong at 800,000. A *Billboard* survey of record stores showed a growing enthusiasm for Brooks's first album and considerable anticipation for the release of his second one. Said one store manager, "The newer country artists—such as Travis Tritt, Garth Brooks, and Alan Jackson—are selling better than George Jones, Waylon Jennings, and Willie Nelson. I think it's because a lot of their hits can actually cross over into the pop scene."

A column item in *Billboard*'s August 18 issue confirmed Brooks's wisdom in performing at the radio convention five months earlier: "Although many programmers were just getting the [promotional] single from Capitol last week, most had already heard Garth Brooks sing 'Friends in Low Places' at the Country Radio Seminar last March and were ready to put it on the air the minute it arrived."

That Brooks was a quiet juggernaut headed toward stardom became apparent in August when the Country Music Association announced its award nominations. The kid from Oklahoma was up for five awards—more than anyone else. He would be butting heads with Clint Black in the male vocalist, single, and song categories. He was also in the running for the best video and the Horizon awards, the latter of which is for an artist who has made conspicuous career advancements during the past year.

Capitol released *No Fences,* Brooks's second album, the last week in August, just over a month before the awards show. Critics liked what they heard. One noted that Brooks's first album "was so powerful that even his champions feared his follow-up couldn't match it. It has."

On October 6, Brooks realized every country singer's dream when he was inducted into the Grand Ole Opry as its sixty-fifth member. Finally, he had aced Clint Black. Black would not join the Opry until three months later, and Brooks would officially welcome him in.

Brooks was now such a hot item that the producers of the awards show gave him his own special stage set on which to perform "Friends in Low Places." It recreated a cocktail party/bar room scene, complete with costumed dancers—just in case the lyrics of the song were too subtle to be comprehended without visual aids. Some in the audience thought the number was terribly hokey and said so, but there was no denying the drink-'em-down power of the song itself.

To Brooks's delight, his role model, George Strait, won the entertainer of the year prize at the show. Black took the male vocalist award. And Brooks happily settled for the video and Horizon trophies.

That night, he succumbed to an impulse that would quickly become a habit. The first time his name was called, Brooks went to the stage alone. But when he was announced as the Horizon award winner, he brought his wife, Sandy, with him to accept. And he's done that regularly ever since. "I'm not much good at it," he announced to the audience, "but when I don't sing, I try to be a husband. This is my wife, Sandy."

Spurred by the awards show exposure and a nationwide buzz that it was something special, *No Fences* sold a million copies within five weeks of its release. *Garth Brooks* had been certified platinum a few days earlier. Suddenly, Garth Brooks was Nashville's golden boy. No, make that platinum.

At year's end, Brooks was clearly in the saddle and on the country throne. *No Fences* then stood at *two* million and rising at a rate of several thousand a week. To show his high spirits, Brooks bought a full-page color ad in *Billboard*. It showed him seated in a wingback chair, eyes bulging and mouth agape, paging through a document as thick as the Manhattan phone book. "Whoa...!!!" said the headline "What a contract! Capitol

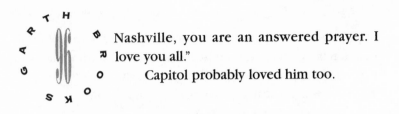

Nashville, you are an answered prayer. I love you all."

Capitol probably loved him too.

GARTH
RULES

As fulfilling as the past year had been for Brooks, it was little more than a token of the successes 1991 would bring him. In early January, "Unanswered Prayers" went No. 1. It was his fourth single to reach that mark, and it stayed at the top of the charts for three weeks in a row.

During the month, television crews were at the Grand Ole Opry House taping segments for the Opry's sixty-fifth anniversary special. For one segment, the producers invited a few reporters and VIPs to come to the Opry stage one evening and watch as members of the Country Music Hall of Fame sat in a circle picking, singing, and telling stories about country music as it used to be. Making up this living scrapbook were Chet Atkins, Roy Acuff, Bill Monroe, Kitty Wells, Grandpa Jones, Loretta Lynn, Pee Wee King, Earl Scruggs, Little Jimmy Dickens, and Minnie Pearl. Roy Clark acted as host. There were only a few dozen people in the hand-picked audience seated in a larger ring around the celebrity inner circle. Ricky Skaggs was there and joking between shots with Scruggs and Jones. Carl Perkins was on hand, as well. Almost unnoticed in all this starlight was a young couple sitting at Bill Monroe's back and gazing as raptly at the proceedings as if they were tourists. It was the Opry's newest member, Garth Brooks, and his wife, Sandy.

A few days later, in another segment, Brooks officially welcomed archrival Clint Black into the Opry ranks. It was Black's turn to play catch-up.

In the Persian Gulf, another messy little war was about to start. Reacting to Iraq's invasion of Kuwait a few months earlier, President George Bush had issued an ultimatum to Iraq's head of state, Saddam Hussein: Withdraw your troops or they will be driven out. True to his threat, Bush ordered the first airstrikes on the day he had set as the deadline: January 15.

Although it would turn out to be a short-lived war, the music industry settled in for the long haul. Fearing acts of terrorism, many executives canceled their plans to attend a major music conference in Europe. A number of performers were equally as cautious, either pulling out of tours abroad or refusing to embark on them. Bob Doyle, Brooks's co-manager, was an officer in the U.S. reserves and was called briefly to service in Saudi Arabia. Still, Brooks asserted he would do the promotional tour of England scheduled for later in the year.

He also volunteered to participate in an ambitious war-support project built around the song "Voices That Care." Written by the producer David Foster, the actress Linda Thompson Jenner, and the singer Peter Cetera, "Voices That Care" was designed to be both a fund-raiser and a morale builder for American troops in the Persian Gulf. The song was done both as a record and as a video and was sold in record stores, with the money earmarked for the Red Cross and the USO. Most of the recording was done in Los Angeles, but Brooks's schedule was so frantic that he had to record his three-line part in Nashville.

That Brooks was one of the relatively few country artists asked to join the all-star effort indicated how much his stature had grown during the past few months. Among his fellow singers were Michael Bolton, Meryl Streep, Richard Marx, Whoopi Goldberg, Paul Anka, Bobby Brown, Celine Dion, Sheena Easton, the Fresh Prince, Debbie Gibson, Little Richard, and Luther Vandross.

Brooks said he was willing to go to

the Persian Gulf to entertain troops, but the war was effectively over within less than a month after "Voices That Care" was completed.

Between the early and middle parts of 1991, Brooks slowly developed into a concert headliner. Initially, he was booked to open shows for the Judds' Farewell Tour, often with Pirates of the Mississippi, his label mates at Capitol, and Ronnie McDowell. The concerts—most of which were in ten thousand- to twenty thousand-seat arenas and most of which were sellouts—gave him a chance to practice his "crowd control." On March 2, with Chris LeDoux and Linda Davis as his opening acts, Brooks made a sentimental journey back to Stillwater, where he packed Gallagher Arena to the rafters.

Although tickets to the Judds' shows were routinely priced at $24.50 or more each, Brooks demanded that the promoters of his own concerts hold tickets to a maximum of $15. This made them the lowest-priced of any major country star. (In 1992, he allowed the tickets to rise to $18—even though he could have filled every hall at twice that price.)

From April through June, Brooks did a few dates as part of the hardware chain-sponsored "True Value Grand Ole Opry American Tour." In each show he would perform on a bill with three other acts from the Opry, including such performers as Minnie Pearl, Holly Dunn, Ricky Skaggs, Bill Monroe, Patty Loveless, Riders in the Sky, Mike Snider, and the Whites. The tickets on these occasions also sold for fifteen dollars each and may have influenced his decision to make his headliner appearances affordable.

Even within the usually blasé music industry itself, Brooks was causing excitement. It bubbled to the top in early March when the Academy of Country Music announced that Brooks had been nominated for seven of its awards: entertainer and male vocalist, single ("Friends in Low Places"), song (both "Friends" and "The Dance"), album (*No Fences*), and video ("The Dance"). Clint Black, who was named to host the awards show along with George Strait and Kathy Mattea, picked up only two nominations.

People magazine wanted to run a picture of Brooks and Black on its cover to illustrate a story on country's hottest new acts. RCA, Black's label, said it would be glad to cooperate; but Brooks's managers wouldn't agree. It had taken their client too long to distinguish himself from the other "hat acts," and they weren't about to compromise the gains he had made. "At that time," his co-manager Pam Lewis recently told a reporter, *People* had "35 million readers, and it was really difficult to turn down. But we felt we had to make a stand to establish that separate identity for Garth."

On March 16, just outside of San Diego, a chartered airplane crashed into a mountainside, killing seven members of Reba McEntire's band and her tour manager. That added another eight to the long list of deaths that would affect Brooks personally. For one thing, the crash was a chilling reminder of the ever-present hazards of the road—hazards that Brooks and his crew were now facing almost daily. For another, the news of the accident broke on the same morning that Brooks had returned to be honored by his hometown. Yukon had painted "Home of Garth Brooks" on one of its water towers and had invited their favorite son to come back for the official dedication. The Yukon City Council proclaimed March 16 "Garth Brooks Day."

Brooks broke into tears several times during the ceremony. His thank-yous for the honor, while clearly sincere, were rambling and disjointed. The local paper had already alerted the townspeople that Brooks's tight schedule would preclude him from signing autographs. Within hours Brooks was on his way to the next show.

To commemorate his fallen musical comrades, Brooks and his own band members began wearing black armbands during their concerts. It was a practice they would continue for the rest of the year. As an added gesture of respect, Brooks dedicated *Ropin' the Wind* to "Reba's 'Crazy Eight,' to their families and friends."

In a front-page article in its March 30 issue, *Billboard* announced that it was planning to adopt a new method for compiling its album charts. At the time, the news meant nothing to Brooks or his fans. But it meant a great deal to his record label—and it would quickly affect the way Americans looked at country music.

The new method, called "SoundScan," would count the number of albums sold by feeding bar code information from each album into a central computer. Most of the big record store chains had agreed to provide this documentable evidence to the SoundScan company, which would, in turn, share it with *Billboard*. What this meant was that album rankings would, for the first time, be based on hard information, rather than on the educated guesses from individual record store sources about what the best-selling titles were. *Billboard* promised the system would go into effect "soon."

It seemed that the busier Brooks got, the more willing he was to make time for good works. In spite of a killing schedule, Brooks came to the Digital Recorders studio in Nashville on April 2 to help out with a stay-in-school campaign. Like the "Voices That Care" project, it involved performers making a record and video to support a cause. Along with more than fifty other acts—including K. T. Oslin, Charlie Daniels, Travis Tritt, Brenda Lee, Barbara Mandrell, and George Jones—Brooks sang the spirited "Let's Open Up Our Hearts," backed by a chorus of incredibly endearing local school children. Five days later he was in Norfolk, Virginia, with Kathy Mattea, doing a free "Yellow Ribbon" concert for the families of soldiers and sailors still in the Persian Gulf.

On April 24 Brooks spent most of the evening walking back and forth between his seat and the stage at the Universal Theatre in Los Angeles. Here he was pronounced the winner in every category in which the Academy of Country Music nominated him. The year before, Clint Black set a record for new performers by pulling down four awards. Brooks took six. His sweep was so complete it was almost embarrassing. Upon winning the award as top new male vocalist, a droll Alan Jackson promptly thanked Brooks for not being a nominee in that division.

Brooks's award-winning glow did not last long, however. Barely a week after the ACM gave him its video-of-the-year trophy for "The Dance," The Nashville Network and Country Music Television told Brooks they would not broadcast his newest video, "The Thunder Rolls." It was, they said, too graphic and violent. At issue were the video's depiction of adultery, wife beating, and revenge. Brooks, in disguise, played the cheater and wife beater who, at the end, is shot by his wife as his little daughter looks on. But even by normal television standards, it was pretty tame footage. There was no blood, and justice seemed to triumph.

Bob Baker, CMT's director of operations, admitted that "The Thunder Rolls" was originally designated as the network's "Pick Hit of the Week," which meant it would be played more often than others. But he added that he was dropping it because of "negative viewer response." A TNN spokeswoman said, "It's a great video, but it doesn't offer any help or hope to anyone in an abused situation." TNN said they would consider running the video if Brooks taped a statement about domestic abuse to accompany it. He decided to let the video stand on its own merits without a statement. Pam Lewis said that Capitol had previewed the video for a psychologist before releasing it and that the psychologist had "found no problem with it." She said plans were being made to combine the banned video with Brooks's two earlier ones and sell them as a package.

Some cynics wondered if the Brooks camp was "pulling a Madonna." Back in December, MTV and other national outlets had refused to show Madonna's sexually suggestive "Justify My Love" video. It was then promptly released to the home video market on its own and became a best-seller. In addition, the controversy earned Madonna weeks and reams of free publicity, even landing her an appearance on the usually hard-news "Nightline." Others criticized Brooks's video for distorting the song's lyrics, which said nothing about wife abuse or revenge. (Actually, Brooks and his co-writer, Pat Alger, had written a final verse in which the wronged wife "reaches for the pistol" and vows that she will never again have to wonder where her straying mate has been. Tanya Tucker recorded the song, but never released it. When Brooks recorded it, he followed his producer's suggestion and omitted the last verse.)

Brooks admits that "the publicists were tickled to death" over the controversy; but he says he "hated it." He had gone to considerable trouble and expense to do the piece. It was shot in Los Angeles over a grueling, stop-and-go, three-day period and cost around $100,000 to produce. That was nearly three times the budget for each of his earlier videos. He and the director, Bud Schaetzle, collaborated on the concept. Schaetzle told one writer that he wanted to go even farther than Brooks did, perhaps to the point of indicating that the man was also abusing his daughter. "But in the end," Schaetzle said, "I think he got a little uncomfortable with that. He didn't want to play that part of it up that much."

According to Brooks, he decided to play the part of the abuser to make sure he came off as totally menacing: "My goal in this whole video was to make this man hated so much that every person in America wished it was them pulling the trigger."

In addition to the public squalls, "The Thunder Rolls" also caused a spell of bad weather between Brooks and his wife. Sandy Brooks told writer Alanna Nash that she didn't like the video for two reasons: "One being my husband playing the lover; two, the abuse in it, especially with the child watching." She says, "We had a tremendous argument on the child watching, and he took it out. But then he put it back in [because he said] 'it's missing that one side of darkness.'" Sandy says she lodged her protest by refusing to watch the finished video.

The matter of Brooks's playing the lover caused even more rancor. Sandy says her husband told her he was going to play the villain to save the cost of hiring an actor for the part. They agreed that there would be no love scenes. "But then they got to California," she continues, "and Bud [Schaetzle] said, 'But you've got to [do the love scene]—that's going to pull it all together more.' He didn't call me when he found that out. He called me later that evening, after they had already shot some. And we had a pretty good-sized fight over that."

"What pissed me off most about this video conflict," Brooks says, "was that every major channel that showed the video put fifteen seconds of the worst part together and showed it. And that was it. The video was put together to set you up to handle this stuff, to make these decisions with the characters as they went on."

To protest the TNN and CMT blackout of "The Thunder Rolls," many radio stations ordered copies of the video from Brooks's record company and held showings for their listeners. The Tower Records store in Nashville played it continuously for four hours each evening the week following its banning. VH-1 then aired the video on its weekend show "This Is VH-1 Country." This, in turn, led to its being added to the playlist on The Jukebox Network.

Even as the video controversy was coming to a boil, Brooks was giving his all to the fans. In reviewing the sold-out show Brooks opened for the Judds in Tacoma, Washington, the critic Jeff Pike said: "Giving the Judds a run for their money on this particular bill was Garth Brooks, who recently cleaned up at the Academy of Country Music Awards. The big-hearted, overgrown Oklahoma kid showed how he's done it, putting in a fine set of rousing rockers and poignant ballads, marked by his charming self-deprecation. On the evidence of this set, he exhibited the poise and talent to catapult him to the ranks of a George Strait." Fact is, he was already there.

Billboard introduced its SoundScan-based pop and country album charts in the May 25 issue. One thing was instantly

PLATINUM COWBOY 107

apparent: country music was selling better than the old charts suggested. And Brooks's *No Fences* was selling better than any other country album that week. It jumped from No. 16 to No. 4 on the *pop* albums chart. That was the highest a country album had climbed in this territory since Willie Nelson's *Always on My Mind* rose to No. 2 in 1982. "The big difference," observed *Billboard's* chart analyst, Paul Grein, is that "the title track from Nelson's album was a top-five pop hit, whereas Brooks has yet to crack" the pop chart. This victory was but a taste of things to come.

In yet another act of charity, Brooks teamed with fellow Oklahomans Vince Gill, Joe Diffie, and Restless Heart on May 26 to do the F.A.R.M. Fest concert to aid home-state farmers. The effort sold out the fourteen-thousand-seat Myriad Center in Oklahoma City and raised $284,600.

Brooks's friend Tami Rose had organized a fan club for him in 1989, just as he was beginning to make a name for himself. One of the main benefits of belonging to the club was that a member and one guest could meet Brooks backstage following his show. By mid-1991 the crowds were enormous, fan club membership was at twenty thousand, and Brooks was discovering there was a limit to the number of fans he could see after concerts and still have time to sleep. He knew he had to cancel that one membership privilege, which was driving him to exhaustion.

But how do you stop the cycle when all those thousands of fans have sent in their ten-dollar fee, expecting to get all the advertised benefits—particularly the right of access? For Brooks, there was only one honest thing to do. He wrote a letter to his fans, explaining why he could no longer honor his initial promise, and directed Tami Rose to send it and a full refund to every member. Henceforth, Brooks's supporters were banded into an organization called "the believers." Instead of having direct access to the artist, they would be served by a chatty magazine that would feature Brooks but which would also carry news about other country acts. And the cost for early subscribers would be only five dollars a year.

It was an ingenious move, and it worked at every level. Not only did it get Brooks out from under an impossible burden, but it also gave him a chance to show his concern for his fans and his complete honesty in dealing with them. And by including other artists in his fan club magazine, he avoided the kind of egotism that makes so many fan clubs monuments to mere vanity.

But if Brooks was shy about blowing his own horn, his managers and record labels were not. To help the world appreciate what a remarkable fellow he was, they bought a full-size, four-page color insert to run in Nashville's two daily newspapers for distribution during Fan Fair in early June. Besides containing a wealth of pictures, the insert announced Brooks's summer tour dates, listed his major achievements from the age of fifteen onward, carried statements of praise from Bob Hope, George Jones, and others, and advertised his cur-

110 rent albums and video. Under the heading "Making Meaningful Music" were the words to "If Tomorrow Never Comes" and Brooks's thoughts on what music should do.

The insert also gave some space to the subject of the recently lambasted video of "The Thunder Rolls." Reprinted was the statement Brooks first issued when the controversy broke. It said, in part: "This video is a side of real life people don't really want to see. I refuse to do a video that is just ordinary. It wastes the viewers' time and mine and the label's money." The statement ended with the vow: "I simply refuse to make a no-brainer video and will do so in the future." So far, he has remained true to his promise. Although it was rumored that there would be videos released for "Friends in Low Places" and "The River," none have been.

A random sampling of Fan Fair registrants show that Brooks and Clint Black were virtually neck and neck in popularity. But in a more meaningful poll—that of albums sold at the Fan Fair record shop—*No Fences* had no peer.

During the summer the Country Music Association begins surveying its membership to get nominations for its awards show in the fall. Fearing that CMA members might not recall—or, perhaps, have even seen—"The Thunder Rolls," Capitol Nashville's president, Jimmy Bowen, sent out "a couple of thousand" copies of the banned epic, with a cover letter suggesting they consider the clip for the music video award. At best, the mailing might lead to Brooks's winning the prize, at worst, it kept him in the right people's minds.

The big story in Brooks's career continued to be albums and tickets sold. At the end of July he made history again. The Recording Industry Association of America (RIAA) certified that, in less than a year, *No Fences* had sold four million copies. Only five other country albums had reached that high a sales level: Alabama's *Feel So Right* and *Mountain Music,* Anne Murray's *Greatest Hits,* Willie Nelson's *Stardust,* and Randy Travis's *Always & Forever.* But none of these had sold as many as fast.

For most rock acts on tour, the summer was proving to be a disaster. And many country acts weren't faring all that well, given the torpid state of the economy. But Brooks was sizzling. "From all my reports," said Tony Conway, the president of Brooks's booking agency, "he is probably outgrossing anything on the road right now—in all forms of music."

Garth Brooks, the package of Brooks's three music videos, was released July 30. Within five weeks, it was at No. 1 on *Billboard*'s Top Music Videos chart, outselling the likes of Madonna, Ice-T, AC/DC, Yes, and the Cure. And within less than four months, 400,000 copies had been sold.

Realizing that Brooks's upcoming album would be a "monster," Capitol Nashville announced that *Ropin' the Wind,* as it would be called, would be priced to sell at a dollar more per copy than other new country albums. The increase did nothing to slow advance orders for the album. More than a month before the album's

September 10 release date, stores had already ordered more than a million copies. Consumer appetite for *Ropin' the Wind* had been whetted by the release of "Rodeo," the first single from the new album. The song's brooding, ominous, and unrelenting sound suggested that Brooks still possessed musical surprises.

Surprise was also the theme of one reviewer, Greg Reibman, who covered Brooks's concert at the Great Woods amphitheater near Boston:

> Radio programmers who insist that a country station could never succeed in the Boston market should have seen the wild reception Garth Brooks received Aug. 8 when he appeared in Massachusetts for the first time since his career exploded in 1989.
>
> About 5,000 country-starved fans (many in striped shirts and hats) seemed to know every word of every song and—according to one security guard—were louder than the throng at Lollapalooza [a bill of touring rock acts].
>
> And those who know the Capitol artist only from his soft-country hits were thrilled to learn that live Brooks is a romping, stomping—and somewhat goofy—showman.
>
> The fun-packed, 100-minute concert borrowed liberally from Jerry Lee Lewis, Chuck Berry, Willie Nelson, and Julio Iglesias. Brooks swung from a rope ladder singing

Billy Joel's "You May Be Right," rambled through the crowd shaking hands and kissing cheeks, and crooned Dave Loggins's "Please Come to Boston."

The remainder of Reibman's wholly admiring appraisal noted Brooks's wide repertoire and mastery of vocal styles. From the time he was able to design and afford his own staging, Brooks was adamant that there should be as few obstacles as possible between himself and his audience. This meant no obtrusive monitors, footlights, or microphone stands. To give himself and his band members absolute freedom to roam the stage at will, he equipped the troupe with headset microphones and wireless instruments. Only the drummer and keyboardist would be anchored.

Advance copies of *Ropin' the Wind* reached reviewers a week or so before the album was shipped to record stores. To one reviewer, Brooks was almost apologetic about having co-written seven of the ten songs on the new album. He said he tried to limit himself to contributing no more than five songs to any of his albums. And, he insisted, there were very good reasons for this self-imposed restriction: "For one thing," he explained, "I don't want other songwriters to give up on me and say, 'He's writing his own stuff.' And another thing is that if you listen more, you learn more. The problem was that these songs just seemed to fit the mood that I was in during the whole albums' creation."

Brooks's producer, Allen Reynolds,

said he had some early reservations about only two of the songs. He noted that he had resisted "We Bury the Hatchet" when Brooks first proposed including it on the *No Fences* album. "I was not happy with it," Reynolds said, "and I voiced that very clearly a number of times. Part of it was that I didn't feel the humor was really coming through." After Brooks did some fine-tuning on the song, which he had co-written with Wade Kimes, Reynolds then agreed that it worked.

"Shameless" also put Reynolds off a bit to start with. To begin with, it was a blatant I-really-love-you song, which Brooks had warned his producer he wanted to avoid. "Garth is a guy who doesn't like to sing, 'I love you, darling,'" Reynolds explained shortly after the album was released. "He's always told me he practically choked on the word. And his songs haven't [concentrated on] that. They've taken a more interesting point of view. So I've told people that—I've related that to song-pluggers. Then, when he told me about this song, and I listened to it, I said, 'Well, you're going to make a liar out of me, Garth.'"

Beyond the subject matter of "Shameless," Reynolds had other reservations: "I was probably a little more confused about it [as a song to be recorded] than he was," Reynolds explained. "And it's probably not a song I would have ever thought to present to him. But by the time he spoke of recording it, he had already been doing it in shows and getting enormous feedback. When I listened to it, I had to admit it was an interesting song.... That's one thing I love about him so much—he's not a one-trick pony."

All in all, Reynolds conceded, the songs he and Brooks picked for *Ropin' the Wind* were the absolute cream of the crop: "We looked and listened widely to thousands of tapes and never found anything that would knock two of his off the list." Even after working with Brooks on three albums, Reynolds said the singer still bowled him over: "He's not one of these big raging egos," Reynolds asserted. "The guy's talent obviously impresses me—it would anyone—but his character impresses me equally, if not more.... I've never worked with anyone who was this fully formed when I met them, in terms of their artistic maturity and sense of self."

Joe Mansfield, Capitol's vice president of sales and marketing, announced that the label had gone all out to give the new album maximum exposure and momentum when it hit the record stores.

Billboard raved that *Ropin' the Wind* was "remarkably focused and cohesive" even though it was not built around a single concept. "The unifying element here," the review continued, "is an encompassing sensibilty that seems to savor all things human without being mawkishly sentimental about any of them. Weaknesses are forgiven; strengths are gently celebrated."

At this point, Brooks made country music history. *Ropin' the Wind* entered—*entered*—The Billboard 200 Top Albums chart at No. 1 its first week out. In doing so, it vaulted past new albums by Dire Straits, Diana Ross, Kenny Loggins, and Rush, and it dislodged Metallica's self-titled album from the spot it had held for the past five weeks. *Ropin' the Wind* was the first country album to reach No. 1 on the "pop" chart since Kenny Rogers's *Greatest Hits* landed there in 1980—after a climb of several weeks.

Billboard's chart analyst, Paul Grein, found something quite significant in Brooks's accomplishment:

> The other albums to open at No. 1 this summer have all been by hard rock/metal bands—Skid Row, Van Halen and Metallica. Such groups appeal to young, active music buyers who are more apt to find the time and inclination to buy an album in its first week of release than are the older, more settled country and pop fans—or at least that has been the conventional wisdom. Brooks' socko debut suggests it's time to recognize that country fans can also be active and committed.

During the next several weeks, *Ropin' the Wind* would show remarkable staying power, being knocked out of the No. 1 spot temporarily by albums from Guns N' Roses and Michael Jackson, but always bouncing back to the top—and selling like crazy no matter where it ranked. The week that Guns N' Roses' two new albums relegated Brooks's album to the No. 3 slot, it still sold 300,000 copies. In country music's not-very-distant past, an album that sold 300,000 copies during its entire life would have been counted a raging success.

Carried along at such a momentum, it surprised no one when Brooks swept up four honors at the Country Music Association's awards show in October. Bowen's politicking had surely helped. "The Thunder Rolls" was voted music video of the year, and its director, Bud Schaetzle, in accepting the trophy, rubbed it in by saying, "I hope everybody at TNN knows how much we appreciate their help."

In front of an audience that included President Bush and Mrs. Bush, Brooks accepted awards for best single ("Friends in Low Places"), best album (*No Fences*) and, best of all, entertainer of the year. During one of his acceptance speeches, Brooks saluted his vocal heroes, "the two Georges—Strait and Jones." He quickly added, "No offense, Mr. President."

Probably because of Brooks's high visibility at the CMA awards show, *Ropin' the Wind* rebounded into first place. This time, it stayed there for eight straight weeks. In doing so, it became the longest-running album by a country artist to top the pop chart, pulverizing the record set in 1969 when *Johnny Cash at San Quentin* occupied the same perch for four weeks. And Cash had had his own network television series at the time.

Brooks's version of Billy Joel's "Shameless" was released in early October and was programmed not just by country stations but by some Top 40 ones as well. Capitol toyed with the idea of promoting the record to the Top 40 format, but nothing much came of it. Given the extraordinary sales muscle Brooks was flexing, the people in his camp showed no enthusi-

asm at all for pleading with non-country stations to play his music. Said Bob Doyle:
"We aren't trying to leave [the country]
base. If it happens, it happens. It's not something we're trying to generate. Let 'em cross to
us this time."

In an interview he gave a year later, Brooks
echoed Doyle's sentiment: "The reason the pop thing
never happened on 'Shameless' was that I went in and
cried and bitched and complained for it not to happen.
I don't want us to court pop radio. I don't want us to
go to pop radio and ask them to play anything. If they
play it by their own choice, thank you, but I'll be
damned if I'm going to ask. If I have to make a choice,
there's no choice to be made. I am a representative of
country music."

Billy Joel confessed to *Billboard*'s Debbie Holley
that he had written "Shameless" as a tribute to Jimi
Hendrix and had tried to sound like Hendrix when he
recorded the song on his *Storm Front* album. "What
Garth has done with 'Shameless,'" Joel added, "has
expanded my perception of what material country
artists can do. Now I'm rethinking my whole catalog."
At this point, Joel still hadn't met Brooks.

On October 24, the RIAA confirmed that *No
Fences* had now sold five million copies, making it the
first country album in history to reach that height. The
next month, it was *Ropin' the Wind*'s turn to win RIAA
accolades. It became the first album of any kind to sell
so fast that it earned its gold, platinum, double-plat-
inum, triple-platinum and quadruple-platinum certifica-
tions simultaneously. In less heady terms, it also meant

More than most country singers, Brooks feeds on the energy his audiences give off. Here he takes a bow at the end of a concert. *(J. Mayer/Starfile)*

The "totally cool"
house Garth Brooks
grew up in at 408 Yu-
kon Avenue, Yukon
Oklahoma. "You could
try things—stretch
your imagination,"
Brooks recalls. "It was
a house you could
make mistakes in."
(Hugh Scott)

Brooks does some be-
tween-songs chatting
before a hometown
crowd as his band
looks on. At right is
his bass player and
older sister, Betsy
Smittle. *(Hugh Scott)*

A*bove:* Brooks in concert in Oklahoma City. In recent months the singer has let his beard grow, just as he did when he was performing at the college bars in Stillwater, Oklahoma. *(Hugh Scott)*

L*eft:* In Nashville Brooks hams it up with Travis Tritt, another of the new breed of country music's multimillion-album sellers. *(Tim O'Brien)*

Right: Brooks at the 1991 Billboard Music Awards ceremonies in Los Angeles. After the show he announced that his wife was expecting. *(Vincent Zuffante/Starfile)*

Below: Brooks fields questions at a press conference in Yukon, where a section of Highway 92 has just been renamed "Garth Brooks Boulevard." *(Hugh Scott)*

Right: Since making his big breakthrough in 1991, Brooks has spent much of his time on-stage accepting awards. *(J. Mayer/Starfile)*

The hyperactive Brooks hurls himself into the arms of adoring fans.
(J. Mayer/Starfile)

Above: Sandy Brooks beams as she stands between two of the most powerful men in country music—Liberty Records president Jimmy Bowen, on her right, and her husband. (*Tim O'Brien*)

Below: Brooks speaks to the news media about one of his favorite causes: Feed the Children. At left is the charity's founder, Larry Jones. (*Hugh Scott*)

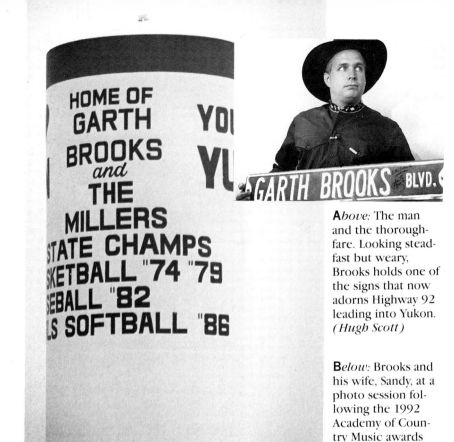

HOME OF GARTH BROOKS *and* THE MILLERS STATE CHAMPS [BA]SKETBALL "74 "79 [BA]SEBALL "82 [GIR]LS SOFTBALL "86

YO[U] YU[KON]

GARTH BROOKS BLVD.

A*bove:* The man and the thorough-fare. Looking stead-fast but weary, Brooks holds one of the signs that now adorns Highway 92 leading into Yukon. *(Hugh Scott)*

B*elow:* Brooks and his wife, Sandy, at a photo session fol-lowing the 1992 Academy of Coun-try Music awards show. He has just won the entertainer and male vocalist of the year honors. *(V. Zuffante/ Starfile)*

A*bove:* The Yukon water tower that says it all. Because of the flour mills in Yukon, the high school teams are called "The Millers." *(Hugh Scott)*

that it had sold four million copies in just under two months.

Brooks was set to play the O'Connell Center in Gainesville, Florida, on November 21, when word came that he had a visitor. The visitor happened to be Billy Joel, who had wanted to meet the country upstart since he heard what he had done with "Shameless." But the occasion called for more than a handshake. "Entertainment Tonight" taped the historic encounter and Brooks wondered if Joel might be up to some piano playing. Joel thought he might be. That evening, Brooks wailed "Shameless" for the howling crowd in his usual emotion-draining way. Then he introduced his new piano player to the disbelieving and then delighted audience.

Amusement Business, a weekly trade magazine that monitors both the American and international concert industries, ranked Brooks as the seventh highest-grossing country touring act of 1991. His live shows, the magazine reported, brought in a total of $7.1 million through the forty-eight shows he head-lined. The Judds, with whom he had toured earlier in the year, were at the top of the list, having generated more than $19.3 million in ticket sales at 120 concerts. Between the Judds and Brooks, in descending order, were Clint Black, Randy Travis, Alabama, George Strait, and Reba McEntire.

"Brooks would undoubtedly be much higher in the ranking of top country tours," *Amusement Business* said, "if not for two points. One, he took second billing on 16 shows as a sup-port act on the Judds' final tour. Two, when he did assume the role of headliner, he insisted on ticket prices remaining at the almost unheard-of $15 level." As one concert promoter explained, "He's trying to get a point across with this—he wants everybody to be able to afford a ticket to his concerts."

By the magazine's tally, Brooks attracted nearly half a million people to his 1991 concerts, a figure that would have earned him the No. 4 spot among the country acts had the calculations been done on attendance rather than income. Of greatest significance, however, was the fact that, when they were all averaged out, the 1991 figures revealed that Brooks had sold out 98 percent of the seats available in the places he played. No other act came close to this level of appeal.

Without question, Brooks dominated country records sales in 1991. Using SoundScan totals, one respected industry observer calculated that the Oklahoman had sold more than 8.5 million albums during the year. This meant that he accounted for approximately 84 percent of Capitol/Nashville's album sales and an astounding 26 percent of all country albums sold.

By every objective measurement, Brooks ruled.

In early December the sudden superstar journeyed to Los Angeles to tape the Billboard Music Awards show—and to pick up five awards in the process. After the awards ceremonies, he told reporters, "I'm taking a flight, in about three minutes, home. Gonna go up on the hill in Nashville to sit with my wife. We just found out we're having a baby. So we are just going to hang out together and be private. This is my first baby. I'm scared. I don't know if I'm ready to be a father, but here it comes."

The puckish round face beams out at you from the television set. "Hi. I'm Garth Brooks," the face asserts. "For the next hour, I'm gonna try to show you what a Garth Brooks is. For a little head start, I'm fortunate enough to play country music for a living. I'm from the state of

Oklahoma, and—*wait!*" Brooks thrusts out his palm in mock alarm, begging you just to hear him out for a moment. "Where're you going? Oh, the country music thing, huh? I know what you're thinking: dull ... [Quick cut to a shot of Brooks clang-clang-clanging the neck of his guitar across a set of cymbals] ... boring...[Brooks crouches over his guitar and scooters himself across the state on one foot] ... old hat ... [an apparently deranged Brooks stands onstage, spastically hurling sprays of bottled water high into the air] ... kind of like watching paint dry ... [two guitars collide midair and explode into a shower of wooden splinters]. Well, all I've got to say is, 'Welcome to the Nineties!'"

That's how the artful Sooner introduced his NBC-TV special—"This Is Garth Brooks"—to America. It was a masterpiece of psychological positioning. It told the wary viewer: All your preconceptions about country music are wrong—let's start fresh.

After working himself to near-exhaustion on the road in 1991, and then discovering his impending fatherhood, Brooks was ready to retreat to his Nashville home for six months of relative relaxation. He could afford it. He needed it. Of course, he wouldn't get it. Superstars can never just turn the spotlight off and forget that the world is still watching them. Granted, Brooks wouldn't have to live in a bus and on stages for a while; but there would still be songs to write, albums to record, awards to accept, endorsements to consider, a nursery to build, and Sandy's health to keep an eye on.

He would even find himself recording for a new

record label. Sort of. On January 23 Capitol/Nashville's president, Jimmy Bowen, announced that the label he presided over would henceforth be called Liberty Records. Nothing but the name had changed, he said. But by separating it from the overall Capitol Records activity, it would focus on the independence and importance of the Nashville operation.

"This Is Garth Brooks" was a compilation of film that had been shot during two sold-out shows at Reunion Arena in Dallas the previous September. The filming was an elaborate and expensive (approximately two-million-dollar) undertaking. Bud Schaetzle, who had masterminded "The Thunder Rolls" video, served as the project's producer. Schaetzle's director of photography was Toby Phillips, an Australian who had worked on the filming of Madonna's notorious *Truth or Dare*. Ten cameras were used to shoot each song from as many as forty-four different angles. Allen Reynolds, Brooks's record producer, and his studio engineer, Mark Miller, spent five months perfecting the soundtrack for the special.

But the real news in all this—at least for those who knew Brooks from his records only—was that the singer was incredibly energetic, good-humored, and musically versatile. All these qualities exploded into American living rooms when the show aired that Friday evening, January 17. In segments between the musical numbers, Brooks, his wife, his sister, his other band members and road crew, and his co-workers discussed what "a Garth Brooks" was and how "it" had developed.

124

Reynolds proclaimed that Brooks was a dreamer who believed in "the wisdom of pursuing your dreams." Pat Alger, one of the star's co-writers, revealed that when Brooks was in the throes of songwriting, "he's like a caged lion, pacing back and forth." In Miller's eyes, Brooks was a resolver of contradictions: "I think you can be a wild party animal and still speak to the soul— if you know what you're saying."

Musically, Brooks took his audience on an around-the-world emotional tour—from the always sobering "The Dance" to the curtain-chewing "Shameless" to a turbo-rocking version of "You May Be Right." Welcome to the Nineties, indeed! Those who witnessed the extravanganza would never again limit their thoughts to rhinestones and "Hee Haw" when country music was mentioned.

More than twenty-eight million people tuned into "This Is Garth Brooks," giving NBC-TV its best Friday-night ratings in two years. The special was the ninth highest-rated network show for the entire week. These numbers boosted Brooks's already astronomical record sales, as well as his radio appeal. *Billboard*'s radio editor, Sean Ross, reported that several country radio stations had taped the special and were using portions of it illegally to promote themselves in their local markets. Ross also reported that two stations, both of which had just adopted a country music format, did so by playing nothing but Garth Brooks's music.

On the Sunday afternoon following the special,

Brooks and his wife were at their home watching a United Cerebral Palsy telethon on Channel 2. As the fund-raiser neared the end, it became obvious that the organizers were not getting the level of contributions they had hoped for. This was familiar ground to Brooks, who had appeared on the telethon before, back when he was just building a name. Impulsively, he suggested to Sandy that they drive the few miles to the TV station and make their own pitch for donations. When they got to the station, they were immediately ushered before the cameras. Brooks said he would personally give a dime for every dollar the local viewers pledged. And toward that end, Sandy promptly wrote out a check for twenty-five thousand dollars. There was a quick round of hugs and handshakes, and then— just like the Lone Ranger and Tonto—the Brookses were gone.

A week later the two had the scare of their lives. Brooks was scheduled to perform on the American Music Awards show in Los Angeles on January 27. The day before, he and Sandy flew into Los Angeles International Airport from Dallas and were waiting for their baggage when Sandy began to complain of stomach pains. Both she and her husband feared she was having a miscarriage. Within minutes she was taken to a nearby hospital. There doctors determined that the baby was all right, but they warned Sandy to rest and stay off her feet. Relieved but still apprehensive, Brooks canceled his awards show appearance and vowed he would avoid other such distractions until his wife and baby's health were assured. Instead of flying Sandy back to Nashville, Brooks decided it would be safer to return with her in one of his specially outfitted buses.

(For the record: Brooks won three American Music Awards: best country male performer, best country album, and best country single.)

True to his word, Brooks cut back on his public appearances until he was convinced Sandy's pregnancy was progressing well and normally. He even resisted the temptation to attend the Grammy Awards show in New York, a month after the Los Angeles scare. Had he done so, he would have been able to personally accept his first Grammy ever. It was for best country vocal performance by a male, based on his work in *Ropin' the Wind.*

By this time, it was virtually impossible to pick up an American magazine that didn't have an article, a photo, or a mention of Brooks in it. He was a pop culture icon. A critic for *Entertainment Weekly* proclaimed: "It can't be emphasized enough: Garth Brooks is this year's (and last year's) primo pop phenomenon, and in fact the hugest pop phenomenon in several years." Even the ultra-urbane *New Yorker* acknowledged its awareness of Brooks with a cartoon. It showed a rather timid-looking man in a clothing store, trying on a black wide-brimmed cowboy hat and a wide-striped, long-sleeved shirt. As the clerk looks on impassively, the man's wife says: "We couldn't know the Garth Brooks look wouldn't suit you if we hadn't tried."

A Music Row wag compiled and circulated by fax

machine an entire "Garth Dictionary." It included such
entries as these:

> GARTHEMOMETER: A device for determining how
> hot Garth Brooks is at any given moment.
> GARTHEOREM: A theory of relativity first summa-
> rized by Garth Brooks in the phrase, "I am,
> therefore you am."
> GARTHEISM: The concept that Garth Brooks is God;
> the official religion of Liberty Records.
> GARTHENOMICS: A system of economics built entire-
> ly around Garth Brooks's willingness to con-
> tinue working.
> GARTHOCENTRIC: The theory that Garth Brooks is
> the center of the universe.
> GARTHESAURUS: A list of superlatives about Garth
> Brooks.

Forbes, not exactly known for monitoring the
arts—and certainly not country music—gave Brooks
the full cover of its March 2 issue. The cover headline
said, "Led Zeppelin meets Roy Rogers ... country con-
quers rock." If the respected business magazine
seemed to be hyperventilating with excitement, perhaps it was because it had discovered that this distinct-
ly blue-collar form of music was generating the kind of
money any pin-striped capitalist could appreciate. The
story cited a study that said that more people
with a household income of forty thousand
dollars and up preferred country music to
any other kind. It also noted that in one

week in January alone, Brooks had sold 340,000 albums, "putting $500,000 in his wallet." (The total was probably higher than that, since *Forbes*'s figures didn't take into account the "mechanical" royalties Brooks earned as a songwriter on each album sale.)

"I believe in the Wal-Mart school of business," Brooks told *Forbes*. "The less people pay for a product that they are happy with, the happier they are with it." The former advertising major couldn't resist mentioning that every T-shirt he sold at a concert "is an advertisement on someone's back." He further explained that one reason he insisted on keeping his ticket prices low was that it gave fans more money to spend on his T-shirts and other merchandise.

All the press and adulation Brooks was getting was too much for *USA Today*'s rock critic, Edna Gundersen. "I say enough already," she wrote. "If some semblance of taste and daring is to be restored to mainstream pop, this hip hillbilly's reign must end. Before the clones come marching in." Gundersen's thesis was that Brooks was the latest link in a long chain of bland popularizers that stretched from the Bee Gees to the Monkees to Pat Boone. He was, she lamented, overshadowing such "worthier talents" as Jimmie Dale Gilmore, Lyle Lovett, and Steve Earle. Brooks was "no musical messiah," Gundersen concluded.

David Zimmerman, who covers country music for *USA Today*, took issue with his rock counterpart. He argued that Brooks was popular because he was "a talented and canny performer" and because "other forms of contemporary music are so poor and mindless, Brooks was sucked into the vacuum." Zimmerman also discounted attacks on Brooks's singing: "[He] isn't the best singer who ever strapped on a mike (Madonna and Paula Abdul, of course, are regular Judy Garlands), but his music has a pulse of real life that even street-hard rap seems to be losing. Add that to the free-wheeling drama of his stage performances, and it's evident that he's earned what he's got."

In his own response to Gundersen, this author wrote in *Billboard:*

What most rock critics either don't understand or won't accept as valid are the traditions of civility and self-effacement in country music. Rock seems to revel in "rawness" and posturing, usually mistaking them for wisdom. Country prefers a more measured and restrained approach, even when the subjects are provocative or violent. The elements in Brooks' songs that Gundersen derides as "safe" and "approachable" are absolute virtues to people who prefer not to be lectured to or shouted at. In country music, the singer is always subservient to the song. Brooks knows that and has benefited greatly from that knowledge. It is too bad that he is insufficiently barbaric for Gundersen's tastes. The rest of us can handle his smoothness.

PLATINUM COWBOY 129

Time followed *Forbes* footsteps, awarding Brooks its March 30 cover to draw attention to its "Country's Big Boom" story. As other magazines had done, *Time* gave Brooks most of the credit for bringing country music into the mainstream. *Rolling Stone,* the oldest and thickest fortress of rock values, summarized Brooks's achievements in its April 16 edition with a headline that said, "With Garth Brooks leading the way, Nashville is booming." Also in April, a *Playboy* poll crowned Brooks best male country vocalist.

In an opinion piece for *The New York Times,* rock critic Dave Marsh seized on a statement from Jimmy Bowen, the president of Brooks's record label, to conclude that Brooks's music might have "a sinister undertone." Bowen had told *Time* that rap was driving people to country music. "For the most part," Bowen explained, "people listen to music because they can relate to the lyrics. If you live in the inner city, where murder and rape is all around you, then of course you can relate to rap. But if you don't share in that life-style, then you can't."

Marsh saw in Bowen's rather straightforward analysis something villainous—a dividing of music along black and white lines. He suggested that Bowen's description of rap was an appeal to white fears, just as Willie Horton's picture had been in the 1988 presidential election campaign. While allowing that country music executives are not necessarily racist, Marsh implied that conjuring up such fears has a racist effect. He singled out Brooks as being representative of country music's politically conservative values. And he accused him of benefiting from a double-standard: "Imagine how the rapper Ice Cube would be denounced for a song about drunkenly disrupting an old girlfriend's wedding and threatening the groom, then setting out on a bender with his crew. That's exactly the story line of Garth Brooks's 'I've Got Friends in Low Places' [*sic*], an anthem for country-loving teen-agers."

While Marsh was correct about country music's historic conservatism, his reading of Brooks's music was appallingly superficial. And even if his dogged mis-interpretation of "Friends in Low Places" had been on target, the song would still have sounded like a nursery rhyme compared to the anger and outrage of most rap classics. Marsh's selective attack demonstrated that he had no awareness of—or chose to ignore—such songs as "The Dance" or "The Thunder Rolls" or the many other Brooks songs that convey not the rigidity and self-righteousness of conservatism but a liberal zeal for openness and justice. (It would be interesting to see if Marsh maintains his original opinion after hearing Brooks's "We Shall Be Free" on *The Chase*.)

Aside from the matter of interpretation, the most significant thing about Marsh's assault was that it showed that Brooks had become, in the public's eye, country music's defender of the faith. The public could not have hoped for a more valiant one.

While critics were hurling these opinions of his work back and forth, Brooks was slowly breaking his own resolve to slow down. In mid-March he made his first appearance on "Saturday Night Live" and then journeyed to Washington, D.C., a few days later to sing on Voice of America's fiftieth-anniversary show. One of the songs he performed was the gentle antiwar ballad "Last Night I Had the Strangest Dream." At the end of March he joined a group of fellow singers and songwriters at the Opryland amusement park in Nashville to put his hand-prints in the "Starwalk" exhibit that memorializes Grammy winners.

As could be expected, the media blitz was fueling enthusiasm for Brooks's concert tour, which was sched-uled to begin June 2 in Denver and end December 12 in Detroit. Plans called for the singer to warm up with four road shows, then return to Nashville during the second week of June for the annual Fan Fair festival. By early May indications were already trickling in that the tour would be sellout. In Billings, Montana, where Brooks was scheduled to perform June 27, an elaborate drawing had to be held—not to win tickets for the con-cert but simply for the right to be among the few who would be allowed to buy them. More than sixty thou-sand tickets were requested for this one event, enough to fill the arena Brooks played in six times over.

Estrellia Entertainment, a company that secured the right to promote fourteen of Brooks's concerts in nine western states between June 4 and July 3, announced on May 27 that every show had been sold out, most in record time. In Tacoma, Washington, twenty-three thousand tickets were sold in forty-three minutes; in

Portland, Oregon, thirteen thousand in twenty-three minutes. The demand for tickets at the various arenas broke records set by Michael Jackson, New Kids on the Block, Hammer, and the Billy Graham Crusade. In Waterloo, Iowa, tickets for a September 18 concert were gone within three hours, prompting fans to ask Brooks to move his show to a bigger arena in nearby Cedar Falls. Brooks refused, since he had already agreed to appear at the smaller site. "He told them he'd play it this year," explained booking agent Joe Harris, "and he's a man of his word. He was going to play it if it was a hundred seats."

Intricate systems were set up in each concert area to ensure fair ticket distribution, and purchases were restricted to no more than eight tickets per buyer. Even so, some tickets fell in the hands of scalpers, who then put them on sale for two hundred dollars each— or more. A great deal more, in some cases. Brooks responded to this outrage in the only way he could. He issued a statement through his publicists that said, "I have seen the prices that scalpers are asking for tickets to my shows. I've seen the show—it's not worth it. Please do not pay a scalper's price."

Under normal circumstances, radio stations at stops along an artist's tour route are provided blocs of free tickets, both for promotional purposes and for the benefit of station personnel. Radio gets and expects this preferential treatment in return for adver- tising the concert and for playing the artist's records. Brooks was such a commanding figure, however, that he didn't need advertising to sell tickets. And country stations *had* to play his records whether they were catered to or not, if they wanted to keep their listeners.

In early May, Liberty's chief radio representative, Bill Catino, sent a notice to country radio stations in and near cities where Brooks would play. It said that as a courtesy to other acts who would be touring in these same areas the stations were not even to announce that Brooks would be playing the region until the concert promoters gave their permission. It also restricted the number of tickets and backstage passes available and said that if the stations wanted any Brooks merchandise for promotional or personal purposes, they had to buy it directly from Brooks's own company. "Backstage is off limits during the show," the notice asserted. The most remarkable feature about the document was how much it kept radio people at arm's length. For lesser artists, radio gets what it wants. Brooks had broken another barrier in insisting on calling the tune.

Following his June 6 show in Salt Lake City, Brooks headed back to Nashville to face the wall-to-wall crowds that awaited him at Fan Fair.

Organized and operated by the Country Music Association and the Grand Ole Opry, Fan Fair is part Oriental bazaar and part rush-hour stampede. The annual week-long event, held at the Tennessee State Fairgrounds, is a valiant attempt to allow approximately twenty-five thousand fans to meet the stars of their dreams—the ones whose records they buy and whose shows they attend. In the past few years, Fan Fair has become so wildly popular that the once-spacious fairgrounds provide standing room only.

It has now become an article of faith in country music that any artist who *really* cares about his or her fans will be at Fan Fair—preferably to meet the fans, pose for pictures with them, and sign autographs. If that is impossible, the artist is at least expected to perform. Each of the major record labels stages a two-hour show at the Fairgrounds' grandstand some time during the week.

Fans had not relaxed these high expectations of intimacy, even for the most popular singer in America. And Garth Brooks was not one to disappoint. Even though he might have justifiably begged off, since he was on tour and Sandy was nearing her delivery date, Brooks chose instead to work Fan Fair as vigorously as if he were still trying to break into show business.

He did all the right things: "Entertainer of the Year? Gentleman of the year might be more appropriate," gushed a local newspaper story. It reported that Brooks had spent more than nine straight hours the previous day signing autographs and talking with his fans. An hour before Brooks had arrived at his booth in a fairground exhibit hall, the paper said, fans had formed a line five-people wide and a football field in length. Authorities wanted to clear the building at the regular closing time of 6:00 P.M., but Brooks said no, and kept right on greeting his fans for another three hours. "Even at this late hour," the news story said, "he spent five minutes with each person."

Liberty Records held its show on the

morning of the third day of Fan Fair, with Brooks scheduled as the final act. The grandstands, which hold eighteen thousand people, were packed shoulder to shoulder. If you were in the stands and looking down at the stage erected on the circular racetrack, you could see Brooks's bus parked a few dozen feet from the left of the stage. Swarming around the bus door were security guards, record company executives, publicists, and sweating TV crews.

Not everyone in the crowd was there to see Brooks, of course. Liberty had an especially strong line-up of performers that morning, including newcomer Cleve Francis, country rockers Sawyer Brown, and heartthrob Billy Dean. Backstage, the gorgeous Linda Davis chatted with reporters and posed for pictures. Lee Greenwood and Suzy Bogguss conferred with their publicists and managers. Liberty's chief, Jimmy Bowen, moved from point to point around the perimeter of the refreshment tent, doing television interviews. Up front, Tanya Tucker was driving them wild with her torrid singing, sassy prancing, and show-it-all black top.

Then it was time for Brooks to go on. The swarm around his bus door quickly transformed itself into a parade that followed the black-hatted artist to the steep steps behind the stage. At the top of the steps, waiting to wish Brooks well, were his producer, Allen Reynolds, and his booking agent, Joe Harris. A very pregnant Sandy Brooks, dressed in yellow shorts and flowered sleeveless top, climbed delicately up the stairs just ahead of her husband and took a seat off to the side of the band and out of view of the crowd. Even though the sky was overcast, the air was hot and muggy onstage. Still, Brooks looked starched and cool in the tight black-and-white western shirt with buttoned collar.

He kicked off his set with "Rodeo." Between phrases of the song, he would look out into the audience, find a pair of adoring eyes to connect with and give them that tight little wave from the wrist that absolutely exudes one-to-one intimacy. For "Shameless," the next song, Brooks laid his guitar aside and delivered the lyrics, hand on heart, as if he were reciting a Shakespearan soliloquy. Everyone in the crowd who had ever been a hopeless, jelly-spined victim of love knew exactly what Brooks was talking, about and cheered accordingly. Still singing, Brooks ambled over to the lip of the stage, dropped to his knees and then lay flat on his belly to kiss one of the hundred rapt and upturned faces. He stood up, still singing, and when he got to the line "I've never been in love like this," he threw his arms wide, as if embracing the world. The crowd melted into one long scream of recognition.

At random intervals, Brooks would bend down to accept a rose, a note, or a package thrust up from the forest of hands waving at the edge of the stage. But unlike most acts, he accepted each offering with a look of profound gratitude. And instead of handing these gifts to a roadie, he carefully carried each one back to a stool and placed it down gently.

After treating the crowd to "The

Thunder Rolls" and the bawdy version of "Friends in Low Places," Brooks walked over to the forest of hands again and plucked from it a pair of tiny pink cowgirl boots for his yet-to-be born daughter.

He thanked the giver and then spoke to the crowd: "I know a lot of you might be wondering how Sandy's doing. Well, I brought her here with me today." He led his wife to center stage, and she waved shyly to the crowd. Then she returned to her seat to watch her husband sing his closing number, "The Dance." When it was done, the crowd cheered mightily, hoping for an encore. Instead, Brooks gave them a long, benign wave, strongly reminiscent of a papal benediction. Then he walked over to the stool, cradled the roses, the packages, and the tiny pair of boots in his arms, and walked solemnly offstage.

His every gesture was golden.

Afterward, he did a brief interview with Cable News Network, during which he casually dropped a bombshell. "My little girl is shakin' me up real bad," he began, alluding to his unborn daughter. "I've got four weeks until she gets here. And … " His voice breaks. "I don't know what I'm going to do after that. She has changed my life, and I don't know if country music is going to be in my future anymore. Because I'm going to be a dad, and I'll see. If I can swing them both, I'll do it; if I have to pick, I'm afraid I'm going to have to go with my little girl and my wife." Brooks had alluded to the possibility of quitting at the Academy of Country Music awards show in April. But his remark was so brief and seemingly off-the-cuff that no one made much of it.

The pressure of stardom on Brooks was becoming obvious; and in the weeks that followed, even after his daughter was born and he was back on the road, his comments would return again and again to the prospect of quitting. From one point of view, there was every reason for him to quit or greatly slow down. He could afford to, and it was unlikely that he could soar much higher professionally than he had already done. Why work like a slave, he must have asked himself, when the best I can hope for is just to stay in place? But there were opposing considerations, too. He still loved making music; he had taxed himself and his marriage to get where he was; and by now dozens of people were depending on him for a livelihood. If Garth Brooks quit, it would be like the town factory shutting down. Stardom had become the mouthful of hot coffee he could neither swallow nor spit out.

Brooks told a writer for *Life* magazine that he had even thought—albeit momentarily—about committing suicide. But from the way he described the impulse, it was more the result of exhaustion than despair. The *Life* layout—which dubbed Brooks "America's Hottest Pop Star"—also reported that the singer was among a handful of famous voices Eddie Murphy had picked to sing on the upcoming release of his "Yeah Song." The other singers included Michael Jackson, Jon Bon Jovi, Hammer, Patti LaBelle, and Stevie Wonder.

Before returning to the tour, Brooks

made a concert appearance at the *Radio & Records* Convention in Los Angeles. He explained to the conventioneers that his band was temporarily without a drummer since the drummer's wife had just had a baby that morning. Because of this, he continued, he and the remaining band members had worked up a set of songs that was different from the one they orginally planned to do. He said he would sing some of the songs that had influenced him along the way. First by himself and later with the band, Brooks did such standards as "Night Moves," "Vincent," and "Mrs. Robinson," then "The River" and "The Dance." He encored with "Friends in Low Places." A writer for *Radio & Records*, the trade magazine that was sponsoring the convention, had this assessment of Brooks's performance: "It might have been easier to cancel the show rather than face a couple of thousand people from the radio and record industry—most from the pop world—with a show created that afternoon. But they loved him. He was humorous, personable and sincere. And, he said later, scared to death."

The much-anticipated Taylor Mayne Pearl Brooks made her arrival in Nashville's Baptist Hospital on July 8. And Brooks—who had carefully left a two-week hole in his touring schedule—was there to witness it. Named for James Taylor (one of Brooks's favorite singers), the state where she was conceived, and Grand Ole Opry star Minnie Pearl, the newcomer weighed in at only seven pounds and four ounces, despite all this baggage. Brooks told *USA Today*, "I busted my butt to reach all these goals, and then something like this happens and you feel very satisfied. The things I thought were the bust-ass important things aren't. Being a dad seems like a pretty full-time job."

Brooks and his managers effectively kept the tabloids away from the hospital, but one got a bit of mileage by showing Brooks holding a baby (someone else's, as it turned out). The headline bleated: "Proud Dad Garth Brings Baby Home—To Tiny Trailer." This "revelation" was accompanied by aerial photos of the Brooks compound, with the trailer in question dramatically circled. Most fans knew by this time, however, that the "trailer"—which was certainly no shack on wheels—was a temporary home for Brooks and brood while the main house was being enlarged and remodeled.

Brooks bought his house on Genelle Drive in Goodlettsville from a former Nashville mayor, Richard Fulton. The best estimate is that he paid $400,000 for the twenty-acre estate. At the time of the purchase, the house had six thousand square feet of floor space. Brooks added another thousand. When the baby was born, the master of the estate was still supervising an ambitious and varied construction project. It included completing a roping arena in a thirty-thousand-square-foot metal building near the main house, and building racquetball and basketball courts. The Brookses had already built the nursery (with a Disney motif), as well as two sunrooms, one with a whirlpool. Garthland also now had a new four-car garage with a patio on top. It did

142

not appear that young Miss Brooks would be consigned to the trailer for long.

After finally determining that he was worthy of a place on American coffee tables, *The Saturday Evening Post* gave Brooks its August cover.

On the road, Brooks persisted in dropping hints that he might pull the curtain on his career—even as he made plans for a world tour early in 1993. "I'm real excited about seeing audiences outside of America," he had told the British journalist Tony Byworth earlier in the year. "But I'd be lying to you if I said I wasn't scared. Probably the biggest arrow that could pierce through this heart is to have my music rejected or for people just not be able to get into my music."

Because country music is largely overlooked in Europe and Asia, many top country acts don't bother leaving North America, where the concert fees are higher and recognition is taken for granted. Brooks told Byworth he didn't plan to hedge his bets by taking a small show abroad. "I had to convince my people that people would not see Garth Brooks unless they saw every member of this organization, his stage, his lights, his whole show."

Ultimately, Brooks begged off doing the 1993 world tour, pushing it ahead tentatively to 1994. The latest word is that he would take off eight months for himself and his family when his 1992 tour wrapped up.

Any reservations Brooks may have about staying in show business seem not to affect his shows—or his energy. In San Diego he hurled himself off the stage and into a crowd of naval officers. In Los Angeles he drew not only a full house but a room full of luminaries, among them Arsenio Hall, Michele Lee, Mark Harmon, Marlee Matlin, and Paul Stanley of Kiss, one of the bands that had most excited the young Garth Brooks. Posing with Brooks for a picture after the concert, Stanley said, "If anything we did influenced the show I saw tonight, then we did our job right."

In late August Liberty Records released Brooks's first Christmas album, *Beyond the Season. Billboard* observed that "Brooks's wholly involved vocal style and keen choice of songs make this album sound like a sincere tribute to the season, rather than the gilded consequence of a marketing meeting."

Early on, the album shaped up as another hit. Record chains had ordered well over a million copies before the first one was ready for shipping. In spite of the limitation imposed by its subject matter, the ever-eclectic Brooks was able to offer a respectable range of songs for the album. To anchor it with familiar sounds, he included such evergreens as "Silent Night," "White Christmas," and "Go Tell It on the Mountain." With co-writers Larry Bastian and Randy Taylor, Brooks wrote "The Old Man's Back in Town," at best a muffled echo of "Santa Claus Is Coming to Town." And to reach a suitable level of seasonal whimsy, he incorporated Buck Owens's 1965 chestnut, "Santa Looked a Lot Like Daddy." For depth and the power of fable, Brooks added Stephanie Davis's "The Gift" and the traditional "The Friendly Beasts." (Brooks enlisted his "songwriting buddies"

Davis, Pat Alger, Larry Bastian, Victoria Shaw, and Tony Arata to sing the various animal parts for "Beasts.") Through the inclusion of "Go Tell It on the Mountain," the singer revealed his fondness for black gospel sounds. As a matter of fact, Allen Reynolds used the same choral voices here as he did on "We Shall Be Free" in *The Chase*.

Brooks saw the flurry of album-release publicity as an opportunity for him to advance his own concept of Christmas kindness. During the same period Liberty Records was beating the drum for *Beyond the Season,* Brooks was tying another of his many good causes into it. Instead of returning home to Nashville as he would normally have done, he used a long weekend gap in his concert schedule to conduct a frantic seven-city round of press conferences for the Feed the Children charity. The four-day whirl took him from San Francisco to New York and several points between and illustrated anew Brooks's compulsion to involve himself in things that matter—even at the expense of his negligible free time.

Before the excitement about *Beyond the Season* died down, Liberty was in the process of unveiling Brooks's fifth album, *The Chase*. It hit the streets September 22. In many ways, it is the best album—and certainly the most adventurous one—of Brooks's career to date. While it is not as rich melodically as the other albums are, *The Chase* is filled with vivid and provocative lyrics. And parts of it are unequivocally political, a rarity for a country record.

From reviews of Brooks's summer concerts, word had filtered out early about one special song that would be on the album. It was "We Shall Be Free." Some reviewers remarked only on its gospel sound; but others noticed it was essentially a political manifesto—like "Blowin' in the Wind" or "We Shall Overcome." Regardless of how it was classified, it emerged as a strong and unyielding statement about right and wrong. Although it advocated such standard and safe American fare as freedom of speech and religion and the eradication of hunger, homelessness, and pollution, it was really a hymn to all humankind. And that "all" embraced all races, women, and gays ("When we're free to love anyone we choose").

Brooks co-wrote "We Shall Be Free" with Stephanie Davis, and it is difficult to imagine a more thorough refutation of critic Dave Marsh's charge that Brooks represented dangerous conservatism. Admittedly, the song offers no program for curing injustices and inequities. But then neither did "Blowin' in the Wind." Both were meant to inspire, not instruct.

The album's strengths don't end with this one song, however. *The Chase* is also very much on the side of women, urging greater sensitivity to their needs in "Somewhere Other Than the Night," revealing the vulnerability of men in "Learning to Live Again," and striking against date rape in "Face to Face." Lest the album sound too much like an exhibit of political correctness, it must be pointed out that Brooks leavens it with songs that are less than dead-serious. One of the best of these is "Mr. Right," a lesson in making out from a singles-bar sleazoid.

Just as the label had done the year before with *Ropin' the Wind,* Liberty used Brooks's newest album to test a price increase. *The Chase* in compact disc carries a retail price of $16.98, making it, as *Billboard* noted, "the highest-priced single-artist, standard-length CD on the market."

As expected, *The Chase* leaped directly to the No. 1 spot on The Billboard 200 Top Albums chart within a week of its release. In doing so it unceremoniously dislodged Billy Ray Cyrus's *Some Gave All,* which had occupied the perch for seventeen consecutive weeks.

Observed *Billboard* columnist Geoff Mayfield, Brooks "accomplished the feat in style, rolling up the third-highest unit count for albums that have debuted at No. 1 since our May 1991 conversion to the SoundScan system. Brooks's sales tally [for the first week], in excess of 400,000 [albums], is larger than the opening-week numbers posted by Def Leppard and Michael Jackson, each of whom had beaten the 300,000 mark. Only Guns N' Roses, who exceeded 700,000 units with *Use Your Illusion II,* and Metallica, which topped 600,000 units with its latest, have sold more in a week than Brooks does with his opening gambit."

Mayfield also pointed out that Brooks could now boast four albums in the Top 20. As this book goes to press—six weeks after *The Chase* was released—the album is still at No. 1, even withstanding the opening-week assault of Madonna's heavily publicized *Erotica.*

Critics seemed as enthusiastic about *The Chase* as

regular fans did. To James Hunter, writing in *The New York Times*, *The Chase* eclipsed all Brooks's earlier albums:

> Until *The Chase,* Brooks's albums overall didn't convey his passions as fully as his singles and live performances, where his spectacular showmanship and eclecticism are ideal foils for each other. By concentrating on the more introspective side of the rock that he adapts to country, Brooks arrives at his most persuasive collection. *The Chase* demonstrates how Brooks combines the 70's singer-songwriter approach with country's understanding of entertainment.
>
> Unlike [James] Taylor or [Dan] Fogelberg, who worked in rock during an era when hits were considered the enemy of noble aims, Brooks tries to draw in listeners; he doesn't want them to have to struggle to get his messages. *The Chase* suggests how, over a short period of time, Brooks has become the most influential agent of something that country music, occasionally to its advantage, loves to resist: change.

Stardom has its pains as well as its perquisites, a fact that Brooks was to learn anew when he awoke on the morning of September 16 to discover that a front-page story in the Nashville *Tennessean* carried the headline: "Garth Scolded on House Floor." The story alluded to a tirade delivered against Brooks in the U.S. House of Representatives by Indiana Congressman Dan Burton. The legislator accused Brooks of insensitivity and, worse, for failing to meet with Amanda Hubbard, a twelve-year-old girl from Indiana who had since died of brain cancer. As it turned out, Brooks, acting on information provided by the concert promoter, had given the girl and three other fans free tickets to the concert, but had declined to meet with any of them.

In his official statement, Burton had said, "We ought to care about kids in this country. And people who are leading musicians in the country and western field and others should be willing to take the time to say 'Hi' to a dying girl. And Mr. Garth Brooks, I hope you get the message."

A Brooks representative noted that Garth usually spent fifteen to thirty minutes at any given concert with the special guest the promoter recommends. Since the promoter in Indiana had given Brooks four names, the representative continued, Brooks could not spend time with them all and gave them tickets instead.

This eminently sane explanation did not in the least mollify Representative Burton's very public election-year rage. "I just get livid when I think about this," Burton told a wire-service reporter. "My view is that he may be a great country and western star, and he may have the accolades of millions, but he's not much of a human being, because the little girl is dead now. I think that is a shame. It's a real shame."

The dead girl's mother was quoted as saying, "For a man whose wife recently gave birth to a healthy child, it is hard for me to believe he could not take a few minutes to meet with Amanda personally."

Ironically, this attack came as Brooks was exhausting himself in his efforts to see that the Feed the Children effort succeeded. Over and above the clear evidence that Burton was grandstanding to endear himself to his constituents, his charges demonstrated how little he knew about the demands made of a star of Brooks's magnitude. Randy Owens, the lead singer of Alabama, told this author that he nearly drove himself insane at one point, flying from one hospital bed to another and attempting to give a part of himself to every sad case that asked for it. He said he finally had to quit or die from fatigue, sorrow, and depression. Brooks was—and is—in the same boat.

Because Burton was so harsh, some observers thought that this might be the straw that broke Brooks's spirit and convinced him to pull the plug on performing for good. Happily, a multitude rose to the singer's defense.

"Of all the weasels in Washington," wrote the outraged music critic Robert K. Oermann, "I think I have identified the sleaziest publicity slut of the lot, the man who recently took legislative time to attack Garth Brooks.... With the nation's education, health care, and economic systems crumbling around us, he grabbed headlines and trivialized his congressional duties by whining about music's biggest superstar on the floor of Congress.

Brooks ... is an extraordinarily generous man, one who has tried in every way to remain humble and charitable. He is the biggest star in the music firmament, yet handles himself better than any of us could in the center of that same hurricane."

Ed Fussell, a television cameraman who had worked on several projects involving Brooks, observed to the *Tennessean*:

> In the five or six times that I have had the pleasure of being around Garth Brooks, I have found him to be a caring, compassionate and kind gentleman.... Another thing I have found about Mr. Brooks is that his grounded and level-headed approach to his rapid rise to stardom includes a conscious effort to remain a regular guy. From what I have seen, it is obvious that he is not willing to be consumed by our often fanatical and consuming hero worship, e.g., Elvis, Marilyn, etc.

Several charities issued a joint press release, commending "America's most loved country music entertainer" for his compassion and hard work on their behalf. The president of the Magic of Music fund recounted this story: "After driving into New Orleans from New York, Garth learned that an eleven-year-old patient from the Monroe, Louisiana, area was unable to come to New Orleans to meet him. He got back on the bus and drove another five hours to go to her hospital room to personally meet her. This was not a request. This was something he decided was the right thing for him to do." Feed the Children, the Dream Factory, the Make-a-Wish Foundation, and the Yukon chapter of the Future Farmers of America also saluted Brooks for his help to them.

Eddy Arnold, a trailblazing star himself and a member of the Country Music Hall of Fame, explained why Brooks is unable to act on impulse when fans ask to see him: "There is another side of the life of an artist, and particularly an artist that is as popular as Garth Brooks is at the moment....It's harder to move him around [a public place] than it is the President of the United States."

Brooks never spoke out officially on the controversy, and it died down within a matter of weeks.

On September 30, Brooks and his wife attended the Country Music Association awards show in Nashville. Early in the ceremonies, Brooks was called to the stage to accept the album of the year award for *Ropin' the Wind*. That it would win the prize was virtually a foregone conclusion since it had by then sold more than eight million copies. Later Brooks and his band performed "Somewhere Other Than the Night," which would become his second single from *The Chase*.

Since he had practically defined country music for the past year, it was no surprise when the announcement came that Brooks was the CMA's Entertainer of the Year for 1992. It was his second time to win the honor. As if

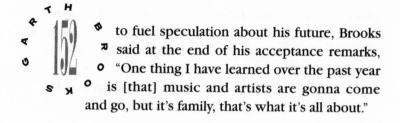 to fuel speculation about his future, Brooks said at the end of his acceptance remarks, "One thing I have learned over the past year is [that] music and artists are gonna come and go, but it's family, that's what it's all about."

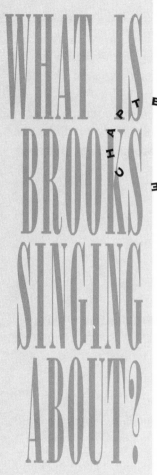

WHAT IS BROOKS SINGING ABOUT?

CHAPTER NINE

You can learn more about Garth Brooks through the songs he records than the interviews he grants. It isn't that the singer is taciturn or evasive. He is, in fact, often quite candid and specific about himself, especially when the interviewer is a woman. But like anyone else, Brooks has beliefs and enthusiasms that simply don't surface during routine questioning. The songs are much closer to the center of his identity—probably more so than even he realizes.

To maintain their careers, most country singers will write and sing virtually anything they believe the market will embrace. This isn't Brooks's approach, and it never has been. He may have been willing to sing any song he could remember when he was playing in the bars around Stillwater; but once he reached the point at which he had to live with what he recorded, he became exceedingly discriminating.

Discussing the pressure they were under to finish *Ropin' the Wind,* Brooks's third album, his producer, Allen Reynolds, said, "Garth and I are both alike in that if we couldn't find [the right songs], we would just plant our feet and not issue an album.... You can't jeopardize the quality of your work just to meet somebody's time schedule." It seems a safe conclusion, then, that every song Brooks writes or records embodies some basic part of his psychological makeup.

Counting those in his *Beyond the Season* Christmas album, Brooks has recorded and released fifty-one songs since he came to Capitol (now Liberty) Records in 1988. Of these, he wrote or co-wrote twenty-two. He also co-wrote the Trisha Yearwood hit "Like We Never Had a Broken Heart," Chris LeDoux's "Whatcha Gonna Do with a Cowboy," and the Branson Bros.'s "Everyday It's Getting Harder to Keep Your Memory Alive." In addition, he has two songs in a regional stage play *Honky Tonk Angels* that have never been recorded: "Crazy Ol' Moon" and "When God Made You." (Brooks, who made his songs available to playwright Cherie Bennett when he was still a struggling artist, has seven songs in the play, five of which he has recorded.)

So intent has Brooks been on recording songs that precisely fit his perspectives, he has sometimes persuaded other writers to alter or amend their lyrics for him. For example, Larry Bastian's "Rodeo" was originally called "Miss Rodeo" and written to be sung by a woman. "I tried to get every gal that I knew in town to record it," Brooks told writer Tony Byworth, "and none of them would. So I'm thinking there should be a way that I could do this. If no one else is going to do it, it's trying to tell me that I should do it. All of a sudden, it hit me to step out of the two people and record it like a third person. And, all of a sudden, the lyric and everything started coming together." That, briefly, is how one obsessive personality came to sing a song about another one.

Brooks also had an eye on Tony Arata's "Face to Face" for at least a year before he found a way to record it to his own satisfaction. The theme of the song is the need to face up to one's own worst fears. Brooks persuaded Arata to add the segment about a date rape and then the victim facing her accuser in court.

Although it isn't on his album version, Brooks added a verse to Dewayne Blackwell and Bud Lee's "Friends in Low Places." He sang the verse (which ends with the line "And you can kiss my ass") on his NBC-TV special, and he regularly sings it in concert. (It is instructive to note that even though Brooks effectively became the co-writer of the Bastian and Arata songs, his name is on neither. Frequently, artists demand co-writing credit—and the resulting royalties—as the price of recording someone else's songs. That Brooks did not—even when he could have done so in good conscience—tells a lot about his character.)

Brooks never strays far beyond the themes he treated in his first album or the images he used to make the themes vivid. Part of this constancy can be explained by his having already had a lot of songs in hand when he signed his record contract. Some of these older songs are just now making their way onto his albums. But even for current compositions, Brooks tends to draw from a fairly limited repertoire of ideas.

The images of storms and bad weather are immensely appealing to Brooks—and not only in something as obvious as "The Thunder Rolls." You can also find either brief or extended references in "Every Time That It Rains," "New Way to Fly," "Wolves," "What She's Doing Now," "Cold Shoulder," "In Lonesome Dove," "Against the Grain," "Somewhere Other Than the Night," "Every Now and Then," and "That Summer."

Just as in the B-movies, Brooks equates storms with passion. In "The Thunder Rolls," the man moves from a scene of sexual passion (with his mistress) to one of passionate jealousy (with his wife). Love, like the storm, is both alluring and frightening—and potentially fatal.

Often in Brooks's songs, the storm outside both parallels and leads to the passion inside. That's the situation in "Every Time That It Rains" and "Somewhere Other Than the Night." In the first, there's a storm within a storm within a storm: Delayed by bad weather in an Austin airport, the singer recalls another stormy day in Oklahoma, during which his chance encounter with a waitress led to a meaningful quickie. The storm that rages around the roadside cafe is a twofold blessing: It ensures that the two will have the necessary privacy for intimacy, and it simultaneously serves as an aural aphrodisiac.

Brooks alludes to other enthusiasms within "Every Time That It Rains." The man in the scenario plays "Please Come to Boston" on the cafe jukebox. This gives the waitress an excuse to strike up a conversation with her lone customer. The talk leads to dancing and, ultimately, to lovemaking. "Please Come to Boston," a 1974 hit for Dave Loggins, is one of Brooks's own favorite songs and one he still performs on occasion. It is the quintessential wandering male song, in which the man pleads—always unsuccessfully—for the woman he left behind to join him in whatever trendy locale he finds himself. Here is a theme with which Brooks has long been able to identify. Also, the customer and the waitress's dancing to the jukebox music is reminiscent of Brooks's method, according to one of his early co-writers, of testing his songs by dancing to them with his wife, Sandy.

(At the risk of stretching a point, one might note here that the waitress signals her readiness for sex by pulling off her apron. In "Somewhere Other Than the Night," a storm drives a farmer from the fields. He returns to his home to find his wife waiting for him in the kitchen—wearing only an apron. While two mentions do not prove that Brooks finds aprons arousing, they do, at least, suggest it.)

The man's first encounter with the waitress is magical. But when she calls him again—on another rainy night—they try but cannot recapture the feelings. Consequently, they agree to just be friends. Passions and storms fade. But the memory of their power lingers.

"Somewhere Other Than the Night" is only incidentally about a serendipitous sexual encounter. Its main theme is that men should be attentive to the needs of their mates. But Brooks and his co-writer, Kent Blazy, use a storm as the vehicle to carry the theme. As in "Every Time That It Rains," it is the behavior-altering power of the weather that forces an unexpected intimacy.

Driven home by rain and cursing his bad luck, the farmer is suddenly forced to face his wife and her desires, which are only partly sexual. Once he does, he discovers that the elements he had just cursed are now enhancing his feelings of intimacy. He and his wife spend the day sitting on the front-porch swing, with nothing between themselves and the stormy weather but the blanket they're wrapped in.

The heroine of Brooks and Cynthia Limbaugh's "In Lonesome Dove" finds her whole life changed by violent weather. She is headed west in a wagon train that gets lost in a summer storm. A Texas Ranger rescues the train, and the lady falls in love with him on the spot and stays to marry him. In "That Summer" the "lonely widow woman" introduces the young farm boy to the art of love, and their lovemaking is described in terms of a summer thunderstorm.

Summer storms are tied to love and lovemaking in Brooks's songs. Not so with bleak winter weather. Here there is always some pain involved.

Certainly there is no romance in Stephanie Davis's "Wolves," but there are winter storms. Like the other storms in Brooks's songs, they tend to strip life to its essentials. The wolves of the title are not only the predators who pull down the cattle helplessly mired in the snow—they're also bankers who pull down the farmers helplessly mired in debt. The implication is that both acts are equally savage and lamentable. Brooks, who did some part-time ranch work during his college years, has demonstrated his concern for farmers by participating in such benefits as Farm Aid IV in 1990 and F.A.R.M. Fest the following year.

It is cold, windy weather that brings up the pain of a lost lover in "What She's Doing Now." It is a blizzard that heightens a truck driver's feeling of separation from his wife in "Cold Shoulder." And it is a "wicked winter's eve" in "Face to Face" that precipitates the discovery that the most horrifying evil lives within one's self.

The clearest statement of how storms course through Brooks's mind was made in his 1992 NBC-TV special. It ended with this message on the screen: "I feel as if I'm a child again, watching an Oklahoma thunderstorm gather in the distance, anticipating its wonder yet fearing its potential. And loving every minute of it."

Sometimes the impulse is noble, sometimes vengeful, but whatever its moral shading, Brooks is a man who sings for justice. In his albums, wrongs must be righted, and accounts balanced. This zeal for doing the right thing was evident long before Brooks and Stephanie Davis wrote their eloquent hymn to justice "We Shall Be Free."

Justice is served in "Cowboy Bill" when the children are proved right, and the skeptical adults are forced to eat their own words. In "Friends in Low Places," the protagonist evens the score with his better-than-thou ex-girlfriend by boorishly ruining her party. The wife in "The Thunder Rolls" punishes her cheating husband by shooting him. (At least, that's her intention, according to the last verse of Brooks and Pat Alger's original lyrics. That verse wasn't included in Brooks's recording, but it was acted out in his video.)

The roles are reversed in "Papa Loved Mama," with the wife doing the cheating and the husband dispensing a particularly colorful form of frontier justice by driving his truck into her and her lover's motel room.

Justice (or vengeance) is slower in "In Lonesome Dove," but it finally comes. In the song, the woman who marries the rescuing Texas Ranger soon has a son by him. Then bandits kill her husband. The son grows up and becomes a Ranger like his father. When the killers return to Lonesome Dove, they have a face-to-face showdown in the street with the young Ranger. And they lose. But here's the kicker: the shots that laid the villains low didn't come from the Ranger's gun but "from an alleyway." Guess who was firing.

"Face to Face" poses two situations in which justice triumphs: a victim turns on the playground bully, and a woman raped by her date faces him down in court.

Brooks is less combative in "We Shall Be Free," but just as determined that right should prevail over wrong. Through its lyrics, he visualizes a just world in which there is no racial, sexual, religious, political, or economic discrimination. "As long as you think the color of skin affects how someone can do their job," Brooks told *Billboard*'s Melinda Newman, "as long as you think who someone chooses to sleep with affects how they do their job, it's not a free country, it's an ignorant nation. The fact that homosexuals feel they have to have individual rights is a direct failure of people to realize we're all human beings. The fact that there is a word 'minority' represents a failure to realize we're all human beings."

In a subsequent interview with *The New York Times,* Brooks further explained his song and used the occasion to strike out at the Republican Party, whose just-concluded national convention had made much ado about "family values." "The song is about choices people make," Brooks explained, "whether it be partners taken in life by homosexuals or interracial couples. I think the Republicans' big problem is that they believe family values are June and Walt and 2.3 children. To me it means laughing, being able to dream. It means that if a set of parents are black and white, or two people of the same sex, or if one man or one woman acts as a parent, that the children grow up happy and healthy, that's what family values are. It's possible to hear the song and not get that message, but that's what I mean."

Brooks was not in the least conciliatory toward those less tolerant. "My thinking is that if I get shot down for saying this, I need to be away from the people that object. You have to do what you believe."

Brooks "previewed" this hard-nosed attitude in "Against the Grain," on *Ropin' the Wind.* In it, the singer cites Columbus, the Biblical character Noah, and John Wayne (who also appears in "The Dance" video) as moral role models. To "make a difference," the song says, "you got to listen to your heart."

The tendency of certain people to act on their beliefs and passions, regardless of the cost, is a theme Brooks returns to time and again. Obsessive and self-destructive personalities populate his recordings. His first single, the autobiographical "Much Too Young (to Feel This Damn Old)," has such a figure. On one level, the song is simply the musings of a rodeo bum who knows he has to run faster and faster just to stay in place and that his obsession is costing him his lover. At another level, it is a perfect description of Brooks himself in his pre-celebrity days. Like the rodeo rider, the Brooks of that period was tired and road-weary, experiencing marital discord and competing against performers who were younger—and, in his eyes, more marketable—than he was.

What makes the character obsessive, rather than just determined and hardworking, is his disregard for the abundant evidence that he is losing everything. Even his own appraisal of his condition is totally negative. This is not a man pursuing a dream—it's a man living a nightmare. It's all pain and no pleasure. Yet there is an odd kind of satisfaction: The character at least controls his own actions. He's like a skydiver—destined to fall, but regulating where and how quickly. This microcontrol is a small consolation within a world that tends to overwhelm, but it is the one factor on which an obsessed personality can always rely. It is the cowboy equivalent of "My Way," but without the smugness.

The same sort of driven character appears in "Wild Horses" and "Rodeo." In the former, the bronco buster is addicted to that brief moment of control when he stays astride the wild horse that's attempting to buck him off. To savor those essentially meaningless moments ("Wild horses just stay wild"), he forfeits his lover and—since he repeatedly breaks his promises to her—even his honor. But when he stops to assess what he is doing to his lover and himself, he doesn't conclude that he should change his ways and act more responsibly, but that he "should let her go."

The male figure in "Rodeo" is fully as obsessed as his counterparts are in "Much Too Young" and "Wild Horses." But instead of initially focusing on the down side of the obsession—long roads, loneliness, fatigue, defeats, and loss of companionship—Brooks, through the song, looks at the alluring elements that fuel the obsession, that sensory bath of sight and sound that's made up of "bulls and blood ... dust and mud ... the roar of a Sunday crowd." Once having done this, however, Brooks returns to the lingering realities of rodeo-ing: "a broken home and some broken bones / Is all he'll have to show."

For Brooks, the battered rodeo rider also serves as a symbol of the dogged athletic competitor who trains and sweats and denies himself, all in pursuit of that one moment of glory when the crowd leaps to its feet and shouts his name. It is difficult to work football and baseball games—much less javelin throwing—into country music lyrics. But the rodeo, with its echoes of rugged, rural cowboy life, is a natural.

In "Burnin' Bridges" the obsession is not about anything as concrete as rodeo competition. Rather, it's the need to always move on, to be a wanderer. Instinct tells the character in the song that he should settle down and cherish the love freely offered him, but an even stronger instinct tells him to hit the road. And like the figure in "Much Too Old," the one in "Burnin' Bridges" is forced to settle for a life of mental torment, since he finds complete comfort neither in staying put or moving on.

Another kind of obsession Brooks examines through the songs he writes or records is the obsession of love. Whether generated by passion or guilt, the love in this category is all-consuming. We see traces of it in "Not Counting You," in which the discovery of an object of real love (or its psychological equivalent) turns the singer's values and behavior around. The obsession is even more pronounced in "I Know One." Here, in spite of being spurned, rejected, and other-wise treated like dirt by the woman he loves, the singer holds out the offer of uncritical and uncondi-tional acceptance. "Mr. Blue" has much the same flavor as "I Know One," although it is considerably more self-pitying. In it, the singer moans of sleeping alone and waiting by the phone. And just like the miserable rodeo rider of "Much Too Young," the figure here ignores the larger reality (that he is at a dead end) and finds some comfort in being able to control the shape of his own misery.

"Walking After Midnight," the old Patsy Cline hit that Brooks covers in *The Chase,* is yet another facet of the abandoned lover who cannot surmount the aban-donment. Instead of adjusting to his fate, he "walks for miles along the highway" as his way of saying he loves her. So pronounced is his grief that he even imagines the sky, the winds and the willow trees grieving with him.

In "Victim of the Game," which Brooks co-wrote, the singer addresses someone who has played the game of love passion-ately but not wisely. Because the victim has acted on the urgings of his heart rather than the counsel of his head, he is left with only "ashes" of the bridge that once existed between him and his lover. And instead of admitting and accepting that the affair is over, the victim persists in trying to fool himself and his friends about the real nature of the split. The last two lines reveal that the singer is looking into a mirror and talking to himself—that he is the "victim." (Brooks also uses the talking-to-the-mirror image in "The Thunder Rolls." The burning-bridges image occurs in the song of that title, "Victim of the Game" and "I've Got a Good Thing Going.")

Brooks's hand-wringing interpretation of Billy Joel's "Shameless" is, of course, the most powerful expression of single-mindedness in love. It is "Not Counting You" elevated to the tenth power. If holding on to this rarest of all loves means that he must completely sacrifice his own strength, standards, and identity, so be it, says the singer. Although the lyrics do not spell out what prompts this volcano of emotion, the implication is that the singer has committed some offense for which he is now achingly repentant. It seems to convey explicitly the kind of regret Brooks could only hint at in the concert he gave the night after his wife threatened to leave him.

While Brooks does not exactly endorse the obsessive personality in his songs, he does demonstrate an understanding and sympathy for it. Moreover, his own conduct is obsessive—whether it be his Herculean and very public efforts to make amends to his wife for having strayed on her or his insistence on being Super Dad to his daughter, even at the expense of his career. Happily for all involved, Brooks's obsessions tend to be more constructive than destructive.

Losing love and contemplating that loss do not always trigger obsessive conduct, however. In "New Way to Fly," Brooks and his co-writer, Kim Williams, give an almost-comic look at those love has "shot down." While Brooks's delivery of the lyrics is serious and straightforward, the lyrics themselves depict characters who are transparently cartoonish and predictable. Instead of sitting by the telephone or walking after midnight in the hope of making contact with their former lovers, these grounded "love birds" are sitting at the bar, elevating themselves with drink and, just maybe, looking for the next Ms. or Mr. Right.

"Like We Never Had a Broken Heart," the Trisha Yearwood hit that Brooks wrote with Pat Alger, prescribes a surrogate love affair, rather than alcohol, for the relief of heartbreak. Essentially, one heartbreak case tells the other, let's use each other to mask the pain of being separated from the ones we really want to be with. Thematically, it covers the same ground as "Help Me Make It Through the Night"—except that it adds the important codicil "and I'll help you." (The song, which begins with the line "Don't be afraid to close your eyes," also plays off the Keith Whitley hit of 1988 "Don't Close Your Eyes.") By turns cynical and compassionate, "Like We Never Had a Broken Heart" emerges as both a tribute to the tenacity of real love and to the sensitivity of those who have been wounded by it. It is a picture of obsession taking a break. "What She's Doing Now" and "Every Now and Then" look back fondly on lost loves. In the former, of course, that fondness is mixed with real and lingering grief ("tearing me apart") that the separation ever occurred. The latter is a more temperate and tender reflection. In it, the singer insists that he wouldn't exchange his new life for the old; still the sound of a song, the sight of a car, and the moments just before sleep bring to mind his old lover, suggesting that he may still be fooling himself. Obviously, the figure in "What She's Doing Now" is fooling himself when he says that he dialed his departed lover's old telephone number "just for laughs." To him, nothing about the breakup is laughable, even though the last time he saw her was "years ago."

It is interesting to note that in both songs the memory of an old love is linked to an awareness of the weather—as if the latter enhances the former. The singer in "What She's Doing Now" thinks of the one who's left "each time the cold wind blows," and there is a corresponding chill in his heart. In "Every Now and Then" the recollection of times past are stirred by a "warm breeze," and the memories are equally warm. And at the end of both songs, the singer is lying in bed "thinkin' what she's doin' now" or "wondering what might have been."

One interpretation of these threads of similar situations and images that run through Brooks's songs is that he is drawing from a rather shallow literary well. A more accurate assessment, however, is that his persistent use of these situations and images reveal to us his way of looking at life and the things that he believes mars or enriches it.

In Brooks's view, love is volatile. It can flare up and intensify itself in sexual passion and it can explode and shatter one's heart and future. It all depends on balance. That point is epitomized in "Same Old Story," in which we are allowed to peer into the mind of two sets of lovers. On the surface, everything looks smooth; but in each pair one partner is just going through the motions and fantasizing about someone else. "Same old story," goes the song, "It's one heart holding on / And one letting go." The specter of one lover betraying the other appears not only here but also in "The Thunder Rolls," "Mr. Blue," "Burning Bridges," "Papa Loved Mama" and "Dixie Chicken."

For an avowed family man, Brooks sings few songs about domestic bliss. There is, of course, a very good reason for this paucity of hymns to hearth and home. Simply put, there is no drama in telling the world how happy you are. And Brooks is an inordinately dramatic figure. If you doubt it, just listen to his soft Clint Eastwood drawl or look into his transfixing, high-beam eyes.

The songs that come closest to depicting happiness at home are "Two of a Kind, Workin' on a Full House" and "Unanswered Prayers." "Two of a Kind" is a goofy, good-time paean to the simple life (as viewed by one who obviously doesn't have to live it) filled with images

Brooks loves: game playing, farming, bubbling sexuality, and family.

"Unanswered Prayers" is less explicit than "Two of a Kind" in specifying the things that make a good domestic life, but more serious in its presentation of the subject. Here is one "old flame" that once burned brightly upon whom the singer does not look back with fondness. She doesn't come close to measuring up to the present love ("my wife") and the rich, but unspecified, "gifts" in his life.

(In spite of his real concern and affection for children, Brooks has recorded very few songs that even mention them. Kids are the "good guys" in "Cowboy Bill" and the eager urchins in the Christmas ditty "The Old Man's Back in Town." Children are vaguely alluded to in "Two of a Kind, Workin' on a Full House" and "Face to Face." They witness their father's rage ignite in "Papa Loved Mama." They are singled out for cherishing in "We Shall Be Free." And one is cited in "In Lonesome Dove." But no child is fully drawn, and no parental views are explored. Now that Brooks is a father, his lyrical subject matter may widen and deepen accordingly.

Brooks is careful to salt each of his albums with at least one comic relief song: "Nobody Gets Off in This Town" in *Garth Brooks;* "Friends in Low Places" in *No Fences;* "We Bury the Hatchet" in *Ropin' the Wind;* and "Mr. Right" in *The Chase.* One reason for this, naturally enough, is to lighten collections that are otherwise totally serious. But another is to demonstrate that Brooks can do more than brood. In all the songs just cited, except for "Nobody Gets Off," the singer uses the songs to poke fun at and deflate himself. In "Friends" he is loud, obnoxious, and uncouth; in "Hatchet" he and his partner are able to relate to each other only by oafishly stirring up old grievances; and in "Mr. Right" he is a singles bar lounge lizard who will say anything it takes to get laid.

"Whatcha Gonna Do With a Cowboy," which Brooks co-wrote and sings with Chris LeDoux, is another pin in the ballon. After romanticizing cowboys by recording such tunes as "Cowboy Bill," "Rodeo," "Against the Grain," and "Night Rider's Lament," Brooks and his co-writer Mark Sanders patiently explain that a modern day cowboy is more of a pest than a prize to a woman.

One of Brooks's more remarkable recordings is so low-key and gentle that it may go relatively unnoticed unless it is released as a single. The song is "Learning to Live Again," from *The Chase*. Brooks did not write the song (although his co-writer Stephanie Davis had a hand in it), but it beautifully embodies the anti-macho pose that has helped make Brooks so appealing to women. The song describes the thoughts and actions of a man as he gets ready for and stumbles through a blind date after being out of the "dating market" for a long time. It treats the same subject from a man's view that Reba McEntire treated from a woman's view in "New Fool at an Old Game." What it reveals is what all men know and generally try to hide from women and each other: that in such situations they are fully as nervous, scared, and beset by self-doubts as women are. This is not a song that Hank Williams, Jr., or most other male country stars could—or would—attempt. But Brooks does it with consummate style and believability.

The theme Brooks most valiantly promotes—and the one his own actions increasingly illustrate—is "seize the day." It first surfaced in "If Tomorrow Never Comes," in which he advises himself and everyone else to treat the people they love as if this were their last day on earth. "The Dance," as discussed elsewhere, makes the point even more eloquently, adding the element of risk-taking. It says, in effect, "Live fully today for there may be nothing to savor tomorrow." "The River" counsels us to float along on one's dreams instead of keeping them at a "safe" distance. Again, it's the "nothing ventured, nothing gained" attitude espoused in "Against the Grain."

If Brooks does quit recording and performing, as he has periodically said he might, it will be because he has taken his own advice and decided to enjoy his wife, his daughter, and his own good health and unhurried thoughts while he still can.

THE HAMLET OF THE PLAINS

You can stand outside of Oz, and you know exactly what Oz is. But Oz is only Oz to those who live outside it. For those people who live in Oz, Oz has its problems."

—Garth Brooks to Jane Pauley

174

Innocence lost is never restored, whether it is lost in Eden, Oz, or Nashville. Garth Brooks recognizes and accepts this cancerous reality, but it still bothers him enormously. How can he come to terms with this debilitating paradox of losing control at the same time he's gaining it?

He loves the crowds and his power to make them howl or weep to his music. He loves the honor he has brought to his family and the stature he has added to country music. He loves sharing his fortunes and excitement with those who are close to him in business or in heart. But the world does not allow him to enjoy and confer these benefits without exacting a vexatious price. Not only must he forfeit the privacy most of us take for granted, he also has to deal with Machiavellian record company politics, the envy of performers less gifted and less rich, the greed of ticket scalpers and merchandise bootleggers, the unrelenting pull of publicity seekers, the pleas of charities and victims who grab for him at every turn, and, most painful of all, the constant separation from the very people he needs to refresh his spirit and rekindle his dreams.

Few artists have been as willing to let the public witness this seesawing of emotions as Brooks. It is not exhibitionism that accounts for this candor, nor is it artful self-promotion. Rather, the impulse seems to be rooted in his determination to be honest with himself and others. And this drive toward honesty may be as much intellectually as morally inspired. Although he has blind spots, Brooks is almost intimidatingly intelligent. Certainly, he can play Q & A softball with interviewers, and he can be the local yokel if conditions call for it. But the man has learned volumes about music, business, and the proper conduct of life, and he has a propensity for examining and re-examining the things he has learned. No wonder, then, that Brooks can appear as moody and as indecisive as Hamlet. He knows that a lot rides on his decisions. Yet he is secure enough in his own identity not to worry if others confuse deliberation with vacillation.

On the evening of the day *The Chase* was released, Brooks revealed some of his dilemmas to Jane Pauley on her "Dateline NBC" show. "If it wasn't for the people that come see me and my love for them," he said, "I would have been out of this business a year and a half ago." Brooks admitted he had been "very unhappy" during this period of his greatest commercial success: "I think I first realized the evilness [of the music business] when the fans started really getting the raw end of the deal because organizations are buying tickets left and right. Then they turn around [and advertise them] in the papers, and they're going anywhere from two hundred and fifty dollars, which I thought was ridiculous, up to seventeen hundred dollars apiece."

However, Brooks continued, it wasn't only the fans who were getting cheated because of his success, it was also his family. "I know my dad and mom didn't have money to give their kids," Brooks told Pauley. "I know that. But the one thing they did have was time and attention. And that made me feel like I was very important to someone. That is what I must give to my little girl. The fact that we have millions of dollars means nothing to her."

Sometimes Brooks feels like he's going to snap under the weight of his show business obligations. During a particularly stressful period of bargaining with Liberty Records on his latest contract, Brooks said, "I have thought several times during the negotiations: Just screw it, drop it, get out. It ain't worth it. It's my little girl that has really ripped my head around as to what's important. It's very real for me. Sandy and I have fifty thousand times more money than we could spend in the rest of our lives. The baby is set up. The parents, my brokers, the whole crew is set up on pension plans. So I can walk away from it."

Throughout his fretting about the direction his future should take, Brooks has been keenly aware that his fans would be deprived if he quit the business. He knows that providing music is a near-sacred service. In an interview, Brooks recalled how important music had been to him in difficult times: "Journey's 'Lovin', Touchin', Squeezin'" got me through a real hard time in high school, and Dan Fogelberg's *Nether Lands* and *Phoenix* albums got me through some really hard times in college. So I depend on music to get me through these times, like [fans] seem to depend on some of the songs we do. I can relate to that.... I still believe the world can change by a song."

Angered by The Nashville Network's and Country Music Television's rejection of "The Thunder Rolls" video, Brooks has since refused to make a video. He is still groping for a way to make videos for his fans without rewarding the people who rejected him. "I think what I might do in in the future—if I do find reasons for videos and do them—is just do three of them and put them on a cassette and not allow them to be released, just have them in stores.... What I really want to do is try and teach someone a lesson.... I'm not going to allow [video progammers] to tell me whether my stuff is any good or not."

While Brooks can seem almost morosely serious offstage, he has a dark sense of humor he resorts to when he wants to relieve his anger and frustrations. Not long after TNN and CMT nixed the "Thunder Rolls" video, Brooks was complaining about the injustice of it all to the writer Alanna Nash. Somewhere in the middle of his tirade about justice and his video that so vividly attacked wife abuse, he remembered a politically incorrect joke about this politically sensitive subject:

"This guy comes home and says, 'Honey, where's dinner?' She says, 'I watched "Oprah" today, and I'm a liberated woman. You want dinner, you fix it yourself.' He says, 'Well, honey, I thought this was the deal: me work, you fix the house and make dinner.' She says, 'Look, asshole, you want dinner, you get in there and fix it yourself.' He says, 'Honey, I don't know nothing about this women's liberation stuff, but if dinner ain't on the table in five minutes, you ain't gonna see me for three or four days.' She says, 'I can live with that.' Well, the first day went by, and she didn't see him. The second day went by, she didn't see him. The third day came around, and she could see him a little bit out of her left eye."

When Nash professed horror at the joke, Brooks responded, "When there is a crisis, I sort of laugh at it.... The thing about the wife is funny to me because I'd never do that."

Whether it's a grim subject, such as spouse abuse, or a detail of conducting business, Brooks lingers over it until he brings order or action out of the chaos. He is the perfect mix of contemplation and action. His brain never clicks off. He told a reporter that he awoke from a troubled sleep with the title for his newest album. According to Brooks, by early 1992 he had concluded that he had accomplished everything he had set out to do and that there was really nothing left for him but to enjoy his achievements. He had already decided by this time to call his album *Let It Ride*. Then, one night, he continued, "I sat up in bed and said, 'You egotistical ass! What makes you think you've reached all your goals? Get back in the chase.'" Even allowing for a bit of poetic license and revisionist recall, the story remains a fine illustration of how his mind operates.

In Brooks's 1992 NBC special, his production manager John McBride recounts the time he saw Brooks return alone to a darkened arena—well past midnight—climb a wire ladder to the top of a lighting rig three and a half stories above the stage, and walk along the narrow truss, humming quietly to himself. Then, as if he had satisfied some strange imperative, he climbed back down the ladder and vanished into the darkness.

Brooks is a complex man, and in his gentle complexity millions can feel the bubbling richness of life that lies below the senses. It is a rare entertainer whose personality is as ennobling as his best art. That is how it is with Garth Brooks. If his journey from Yukon to Oz has caused him some suffering—well, that goes with the territory.

He could have missed the pain, but he'd have had to miss the dance.

DISCOGRAPHY

ALBUMS BY GARTH BROOKS

Garth Brooks (1989)/Capitol Records

    "Not Counting You" (Garth Brooks)*

    "I've Got a Good Thing Going" (Larry Bastian, Sandy Mahl, Garth Brooks)

    "If Tomorrow Never Comes" (Kent Blazy, Garth Brooks)*

    "Everytime That It Rains" (Charley Stefl, Ty England, Garth Brooks)

    "Alabama Clay" (Larry Cordle, R. Scaife)

    "Much Too Young (to Feel This Damn Old)" (Randy Taylor, Garth Brooks)*

    "Cowboy Bill" (Larry Bastian, Ed Berghoff)

    "Nobody Gets Off in This Town" (Larry Bastian, Dewayne Blackwell)

* Released as singles as of November 12, 1992

"I Know One" (Jack Clement)

"The Dance" (Tony Arata)*

No Fences (1990)/Capitol/Nashville Records

"The Thunder Rolls" (Pat Alger, Garth Brooks)*

"New Way to Fly" (Kim Williams, Garth Brooks)

"Two of a Kind, Workin' on a Full House" (Bobby Boyd, Warren Dale Haynes, Dennis Robbins)*

"Victim of the Game" (Mark D. Sanders, Garth Brooks)

"Friends in Low Places" (Dewayne Blackwell, Bud Lee)*

"Wild Horses" (Bill Shore, David Wills)

"Unanswered Prayers" (Pat Alger, Larry Bastian)*

"Same Old Story" (Tony Arata)

"Mr. Blue" (Dewayne Blackwell)

"Wolves" (Stephanie Davis)

Ropin' the Wind (1991)/Liberty Records

"Against the Grain" (Bruce Bouton, Larry Cordle, Carl Jackson)

"Rodeo" (Larry Bastian)*

"What She's Doing Now" (Pat Alger, Garth Brooks)*

"Burnin' Bridges" (Stephanie C. Brown, Garth Brooks)

"Papa Loved Mama" (Ken Williams, Garth Brooks)*

"Shameless" (Billy Joel)*

"Cold Shoulder" (Kent Blazy, Kim Williams, Garth Brooks)

"We Bury the Hatchet" (Wade Kimes, Garth Brooks)

"In Lonesome Dove" (Cynthia Limbaugh, Garth Brooks)

"The River" (Victoria Shaw, Garth Brooks)*

Beyond the Season (1992)/Liberty Records

"Go Tell It on the Mountain" (Traditional)

"God Rest Ye Merry Gentlemen" (Traditional)

"The Old Man's Back in Town" (Larry Bastian, Randy Taylor, Garth Brooks)

"The Gift" (Stephanie Davis)

"Unto You This Night" (Steve Gillette, Rex Benson)

"White Christmas" (Irving Berlin)

"The Friendly Beasts" (Traditional)

"Santa Looked a Lot Like Daddy" (Buck Owens, Don Rich)

"Silent Night" (Traditional)

"Mary's Dream" (Bobby Wood, Mark Casstevens)

"What Child Is This" (Traditional)

The Chase (1992)/Liberty Records

"We Shall Be Free" (Stephanie Davis, Garth Brooks)*

"Somewhere Other Than the Night" (Kent Blazy, Garth Brooks)*

"Mr. Right" (Garth Brooks)

"Every Now and Then" (Buddy Mondlock, Garth Brooks)

"Walking After Midnight" (Alan Block, Don Hecht)

"Dixie Chicken" (Lowell George, Martin Kibbee)

"Learning to Live Again" (Stephanie Davis, Don Schlitz)

"That Summer" (Pat Alger, Garth Brooks, Sandy Mahl)

"Night Rider's Lament" (Mike Burton)

"Face to Face" (Tony Arata)

GARTH BROOKS ON OTHER ALBUMS
(singing harmony)
Trisha Yearwood: *Trisha Yearwood* (1991)/MCA Records

"Like We Never Had a Broken Heart" (Pat Alger, Garth Brooks)*

"Victim of the Game" (Garth Brooks, Mark D. Sanders)

Martina McBride: *The Time Has Come* (1992)/ RCA Records

"Cheap Whiskey" (Emory Gordy, Jr., Jim Rushing)*

Chris LeDoux: *Whatcha Gonna Do With a Cowboy* (1992)/Liberty Records

"Whatcha Gonna Do With a Cowboy" (Garth Brooks, Mark D. Sanders)*

183

 GARTH BROOKS

Trisha Yearwood: *Hearts in Armor* (1992)/MCA Records

"Nearest Distant Shore" (Gary Harrison, Tim Mensy)

George Jones: *Walls Can Fall* (1992)/MCA Records

"I Don't Need Your Rockin' Chair"

CHRONOLOGY

Note: *Billboard* is the basis for all chart positions listed.

1962
February 7: Garth Brooks born in Tulsa, Oklahoma.

1966
March: Brooks family moves to Yukon, Oklahoma.

1978
February 7: Brooks gets a banjo for his sixteenth birthday.

1980
Brooks graduates from Yukon High School and enrolls at Oklahoma State University in Stillwater.

1981
May: George Strait's first single, "Unwound," is released. In Yukon, Brooks hears the song and decides he might like to be a country singer.

1982

April 6: Representing Iba Hall, an athletic-dorm at OSU, Brooks wins the fifty-dollar first prize in a talent show sponsored by the Active Cultural Experiences for Students Committee of the Residence Halls Association.

1984

December: Brooks graduates from OSU with a degree in marketing.

1985

Brooks makes his first trip to Nashville. It lasts one day.

1986

May 24: Brooks marries Sandy Mahl.

1987

May 29: Brooks accepted into ASCAP after having applied earlier this month.

Late summer: Brooks returns to Nashville with Sandy and members of his band.

1988

February: Bob Doyle leaves ASCAP to set up his publishing company, Major Bob Music. Garth Brooks is one of the first two writers signed. The other is Larry Bastian, writer of "Rodeo." Not long after this, Doyle and publicist Pam Lewis form Doyle/Lewis Management, with Brooks as a client.

March 23: Bob Doyle, Brooks's co-manager, asks Capitol Records' chief, Jim Foglesong, to set up an appointment to listen to Brooks.

April 4: Brooks performs for Foglesong and his vice
president of A & R, Lynn Shults, at the Capitol
Records office in Nashville.

May 11: Shults sees Brooks perform at the Bluebird
Cafe and makes a handshake agreement to sign
him to a recording contract.

June 17: Brooks officially signs with Capitol Records.

1989

Month uncertain: Tami Rose forms Garth Brooks Fan
Club.

March 25: "Much Too Young (to Feel This Damn Old)"
debuts at No. 94 on Billboard's country singles
chart. It peaks at No. 8 on July 15.

April 12: *Garth Brooks,* Brooks's first album, released.

May: Brooks goes on the road to promote the album.

May 9: Keith Whitley dies of an alcohol overdose. He
will later be honored in Brooks's "The Dance"
video.

June 10: Clint Black's first single, "A Better Man," goes
to No. 1 on the charts. For the next year, Black is
Brooks's chief opposition and the one by whom
he measures his own achievements.

July 21: Video of "If Tomorrow Never Comes" completed.

September 9: "If Tomorrow Never Comes" debuts on
the charts.

October 21: Brooks sings "The Dance" on The
Nashville Network's police series pilot
"Nashville Beat."

November 4: Sandy Brooks gives her hus-

PLATINUM COWBOY 187

band the "my way or the highway"
ultimatum.

November 5: Brooks breaks down onstage
at Cape Girardeau, Missouri, during a
concert, but he recovers and wins over the
house.

December 9: "If Tomorrow Never Comes" becomes
Brooks's first No. 1 single.

December 11: Jimmy Bowen takes command of Capitol
Records and fires virtually the whole staff, including the ones who signed and promoted Brooks.

1990

January 20: "Not Counting You" debuts on the charts.
It peaks at No. 2 on April 7.

March: Joe Mansfield named vice president of sales and
marketing at Capitol/Nashville Records. He will
be instrumental in making Brooks a multimillion
seller.

March 2: Brooks sings for disc jockeys at the ASCAP-
sponsored luncheon at the Country Radio
Seminar.

April: Kelly Brooks joins his brother's road crew as
"money man."

April 7: Brooks sings at Farm Aid IV at the Hoosier
Dome in Indianapolis.

April 8: Young AIDS victim Ryan White dies in
Indianapolis shortly after Elton John leaves his bedside to perform at Farm Aid. John plays "Candle in
the Wind" and dedicates it to White.

April 24: Brooks and Chris LeDoux meet for the first
time when they perform on the same bill at the

Cocky Bull in Victorville, California.

April 25: Up for top new male vocalist, top song, and top single at the Academy of Country Music Awards, Brooks loses in all three categories—and to Clint Black in two of them. Black wins four ACM awards, more than any newcomer in the academy's history.

May: Brooks tapes "The Dance" video at Scene Three in Nashville. The video becomes his first step toward superstardom.

May 5: "The Dance" debuts on the charts.

June 6: Brooks makes his first singing appearance at Fan Fair, performing on the Capitol Records show. During the show, Capitol Records president Jimmy Bowen presents Brooks with his first gold album, which signifies that *Garth Brooks* has sold 500,000 copies.

July 21: "The Dance" becomes Brooks's second No. 1 hit. It stays No. 1 for two weeks.

July 22: Brooks sings at Jamboree in the Hills.

August 18: "Friends in Low Places" debuts on the charts.

August 27: Brooks's second album, *No Fences,* released.

October 4: *Garth Brooks* certified platinum (one million copies sold).

October 6: Brooks joins the Grand Ole Opry as its sixty-fifth member. "Friends in Low Places" becomes Brooks's third No. 1 hit. It stays No. 1 for four weeks.

October 8: Brooks wins the Country Music

Association's Horizon award and best video award for "The Dance."

October 9: *No Fences* certified platinum.

October 10: Brooks's "If Tomorrow Never Comes"and "Much Too Young (to Feel This Damn Old)" win ASCAP awards.

October 13: Brooks plays to more than fifty thousand people at the Dallas State Fair.

October 16: Brooks makes his first "Tonight Show" appearance.

November 3: "Unanswered Prayers" debuts on the charts.

November 18-21: Brooks does a media tour of London.

November 22: Brooks rides in Macy's Thanksgiving Day Parade.

1991

January 12: "Unanswered Prayers" becomes Brooks's fourth No. 1 single. It stays No. 1 for three weeks.

January 15: The United States launches its first air strikes on Iraq in Operation Desert Storm.

February 2: "Two of a Kind (Workin' on a Full House)" debuts on charts. (Dennis Robbins, who co-wrote the song, had released it himself as a single in 1987 on MCA Records. His single rose to only No. 71 on the charts.)

February 10: Brooks records for the "Voices That Care" project in support of U.S. troops in the Persian Gulf.

February 27: U.S. ground war with Iraq ends.

March 16: Seven members of Reba McEntire's band and her road manager are killed in a plane crash near

San Diego. From this date until December 15, Brooks and his band wear black armbands onstage to honor the dead.

Brooks returns to Yukon to be honored with his own "Garth Brooks Day," a ceremony that includes the official dedication of a sign on one of the town's water towers that proclaims: "Home of Garth Brooks."

April 2: Brooks joins dozens of other country artists to record the "Let's Open Up Our Hearts" single and video to benefit schoolchildren.

April 6: "Two of a Kind (Workin' on a Full House)" becomes Brooks's fifth No. 1 single.

April 7: Brooks and Kathy Mattea give a free "Yellow Ribbon" concert in Norfolk, Virginia, to salute the families of those serving in Operation Desert Storm.

April 29: Brooks sweeps the Academy of Country Music Awards Show, winning the entertainer, male vocalist, album (*No Fences*), single ("Friends in Low Places"), song, and video ("The Dance") categories.

May 1: Country Music Television drops Brooks's "The Thunder Rolls" video from its playlist, and the Nashville Network announces it won't play the video.

May 6-11: The Tower Records store in Nashville plays the "Thunder Rolls" video 4 to 8 P.M. daily.

May 18: "The Thunder Rolls" debuts on the charts.

PLATINUM 191 COWBOY

May 25: *Billboard* institutes the SoundScan record-sales-monitoring system, which will work to Brooks's advantage when his third album is released later in the year.

May 26: Brooks plays the F.A.R.M. Fest '91 benefit for farmers in Oklahoma City.

June 22: "The Thunder Rolls" becomes Brooks's sixth No. 1 single. It stays No. 1 for two weeks.

July: Capitol/Nashville mails copies of the "Thunder Rolls" video to "a couple of thousand" Country Music Association members, asking them to consider voting for it as the year's best country video.

August 17: "Rodeo" debuts on the charts, peaking at No. 3 on October 5.

September 10: *Ropin' the Wind,* Brooks's third album, released. It is the first country album to carry a $10.98 suggested retail price.

September 20-21: Brooks's two sold-out concerts at Reunion Arena in Dallas are filmed for the upcoming NBC-TV special, "This Is Garth Brooks." Trisha Yearwood and Chris LeDoux are Brooks's opening acts.

September 28: *Ropin' the Wind* debuts at No. 1 on The Billboard Top 200 Albums chart, dislodging Metallica, which had held the top position for two weeks, and towering over new albums by Dire Straits, Tesla, Kenny Loggins, and Diana Ross, which also made their chart debuts that same week.

October 2: Brooks wins Country Music Association

awards for entertainer of the year, album (*No Fences*), single ("Friends in Low Places") and music video ("The Thunder Rolls"). He jokes with President George Bush, who is in the audience.

October 19: "Shameless" debuts on the charts.

October 25: Brooks appears on CBS-TV's "Walt Disney World Twentieth Anniversary Special."

November 2: Brooks plays himself on the NBC-TV situation comedy "Empty Nest."

November 16: "Shameless" becomes Brooks's seventh No. 1 hit after just five weeks on the charts. It stays at No. 1 for two weeks.

November 21: Brooks meets Billy Joel for first time in Gainesville, Florida, when the singer and writer of "Shameless" makes a surprise appearance at Brooks's sold-out concert at the O'Connell Center. Joel plays piano when Brooks sings "Shameless" and only then is introduced to the crowd.

December 3: Brooks tapes the "Billboard Music Awards" show in Santa Monica for broadcast December 9 on the Fox Network. He wins five awards: top albums artist, top country singles artist, top country album (*No Fences*), top country albums artist, and top country artist.

December 11: *Honky Tonk Angels,* a play written by Cherie Bennett and containing seven Garth Brooks songs, opens at Jonathan's Uptown in Charlotte, North Carolina. One of the main characters in the production is played by Carrie Folks, who is managed by Doyle/Lewis, which also man-

ages Brooks. The songs are "Much Too Young (to Feel This Damn Old)," "Burnin' Bridges," "If Tomorrow Never Comes," "Victim of the Game," "The River," and the still-unrecorded "Crazy Ol' Moon" and "When God Made You."

December 15: Brooks and his band discontinue wearing the black armbands they have worn all year to honor the eight members of Reba McEntire's entourage killed in a plane crash March 16.

December 26: Brooks is featured on the syndicated TV special *Entertainers '91,* hosted by Dennis Miller. (Date indicates when program aired in Nashville.)

December 27: Brooks's "The Dance" video featured in the CBS- TV special "The Meaning of Life," hosted by George Burns. Brooks listed as *Entertainment Weekly*'s No. 2 entertainer of the year, coming in second to director/actress Jodie Foster.

1992

January 4: "What She's Doing Now" debuts on the charts.

January 17: Brooks's NBC-TV special "This Is Garth Brooks" broadcasts.

January 19: Garth and Sandy Brooks make a surprise visit to WKRN-TV in Nashville, where a two-day telethon for United Cerebral Palsy is winding down, and present the charity a personal check for twenty-five thousand dollars.

January 23: Capitol/Nashville, Brooks's record label, changes its name to Liberty Records.

January 26: Sandy Brooks becomes ill in Los Angeles

and has to be hospitalized. There is fear she will lose her baby.

January 27: Brooks wins American Music Awards for best country male performer, best country album (*No Fences*), and best country single ("The Thunder Rolls").

February 1: "Papa Loved Mama" debuts on the charts, peaking at No. 3 on May 16.

February 15: "What She's Doing Now" becomes Brooks's eighth No. 1 single. It stays at No. 1 for four weeks.

February 25: Brooks wins his first Grammy award— best vocal performance by a male country artist— for *Ropin' the Wind.*

March 1: Brooks's fan club opens the 1-900-GET GARTH information hotline.

March 2: Brooks appears on the cover of *Forbes.*

March 5: Brooks packs the Roy Acuff Theatre at Opryland for his "Super Faces" show for the Country Radio Seminar.

March 17: Brooks wins People Choice Awards as best male country performer and best male musical performer.

March 14: Brooks appears on "Saturday Night Live."

March 18: Brooks is given the first ASCAP "Voice of Music" award during the grand-opening cere- monies of ASCAP's new Nashville offices.

March 21: Brooks sings on the Voice of Amer- ica's fiftieth anniversary show from Washington, D.C.

March 23: Brooks appears on the cover of *Time.*

PLATINUM COWBOY 195

March 31: Brooks memorialized in the "Starwalk" outside the Roy Acuff Theatre at Opryland, USA. The attraction honors country artists who have won Grammys.

April: Brooks named best male country vocalist in *Playboy*'s music poll.

April 27: EMI releases Brooks's single "What She's Doing Now"/ "Shameless" in England.

April 29: Brooks is named the Academy of Country Music's entertainer and male vocalist of the year.

May 5: "The River" debuts on the charts.

May 31: Yukon designates the stretch of Highway 92 from the Interstate 40 exit to Main Street as "Garth Brooks Boulevard."

June 2: Brooks begins his 1992 tour at McNichols Arena in Denver.

June 10: Brooks performs on the Liberty Records show at Fan Fair.

July 8: Taylor Mayne Pearl Brooks, Garth and Sandy's first child, born in Nashville.

July 17: *Entertainment Weekly*'s survey proclaims Brooks America's favorite male singer. He outpolls Michael Bolton, Bruce Springsteen, Luther Vandross, and Phil Collins.

July 25: "The River" becomes Brooks's ninth No. 1 single.

August: Brooks's photo is on the cover of the *Saturday Evening Post.*

August 13: Brooks is nominated for entertainer, male vocalist, and album of the year by the Country Music Association.

August 25: Liberty releases *Beyond the Season,*
Brooks's first Christmas album, and "We Shall Be
Free," the first single from *The Chase.* The week
following its release, the album goes to No. 5 on
The Billboard Top 200 Albums chart and to No. 2
on the Top Country Albums chart.

September 5: "We Shall Be Free" enters the chart.

September 10: U.S. Congressman Dan Burton, a
Republican from Indiana, condemns Brooks in a
speech in the House of Representatives for failing
to meet personally with a fan, Amanda Hubbard,
who was dying of cancer. The music community
rallies to Brooks's defense, characterizing him as
one of the most involved and caring persons in
the entertainment business.

September 22: Liberty releases *The Chase,* Brooks's
fifth album. The following week the album goes
to No. 1 on both the Billboard Top 200 Albums
and Top Country Albums charts.

September 30: Brooks wins the Country Music
Association's entertainer of the year and album of
the year (for *Ropin' the Wind*) awards. He performs "Somewhere Other Than the Night" on the
awards show.

October 3: *The Chase* makes its debut at No. 1 on The
Billboard Top 200 Albums chart, dislodging Billy
Ray Cyrus's *Some Gave All,* which had occupied
the spot for seventeen straight weeks.

October 26: "Somewhere Other Than the
Night" released

October 30: *Entertainment Weekly* lists
Brooks as forty-second in rank on its

GARTH BROOKS 198

list of the 101 most influential entertainment figures.

"We Shall Be Free" peaks at No.
12 on Billboard's country chart. It is the
only Brooks single to date to fail to make
the Top 10. Taking note of the song's early death,
some reporters begin speculating that its message
of tolerance was "too liberal" for country audiences.

November 6: "The Old Man's Back in Town," from
Brooks's Christmas album, released.